JOHN CAGE

AMERICAN

Composers

A list of books in the series
appears at the end of this volume.

John
Cage

David Nicholls

UNIVERSITY OF

ILLINOIS PRESS

Urbana and Chicago

Library of Congress Cataloging-in-Publication Data

Nicholls, David, 1955–

John Cage / David Nicholls.

p.   cm. — (American composers)

Includes bibliographical references (p.), discography (p.),
and index.

ISBN-13 978-0-252-03215-8 (cloth : alk. paper)

ISBN-10 0-252-03215-2 (cloth : alk. paper)

1. Cage, John. 2. Composers—United States—Biography.
I. Title.

ML410.C24N53   2007

780.92—dc22   2007011378

For T, B, D, P, and H†

John Cage outside the Windfall Dutch Barn at Salt Springsville, New York, summer 1983. Photograph by John Mazarak. Courtesy of John Mazarak.

I once asked Arragon, the historian, how history was written.
He said, "You have to invent it."

—John Cage, "An Autobiographical Statement," 1989.

                My
             mEmory
         of whaT
                Happened
            is nOt
    what happeneD

—John Cage, "Composition in Retrospect," 1983/88,
opening mesostic.

CONTENTS

PRELUDE

March 1943. Museum of Modern Art, New York City

A group of musicians, in formal concert attire, waits expectantly for the conductor's downbeat. The conductor is a tall, smiling, thirty-year-old Californian. As his baton descends, the musicians start to play their instruments, which are entirely percussive: thunder sheets, temple gongs, oxen bells, cymbals, anvils, orchestral bells, and automobile brake drums.

August 1952. Maverick Concert Hall, Woodstock, New York

A pianist walks onto the stage, sits down at the piano, and closes the keyboard cover. Thirty seconds later, he opens the cover. He repeats this sequence of actions twice: all that changes is the length of time—two minutes, twenty-three seconds; then one minute, forty seconds—between closing and opening the lid. After the final opening of the lid, he stands and takes his bow.

March 1968. Ryerson Polytechnical Institute, Toronto

Two men sit in easy chairs. Between them is a table, on which are placed glasses of wine and a chessboard. The game commences. As each player moves his pieces, the initial silence is progressively intruded upon until—at the game's midpoint—the room is filled with amplified noises. As pieces are taken, and the confrontation moves toward its conclusion, the sound levels gradually diminish.

||||

It is events like those described above—performances of the *First Construction (in Metal)* (1939), *4' 33"* (1952), and *Reunion* (1968), respectively—that have defined

1

public awareness of the work of John Cage (1912–92) and to a considerable extent contributed to the misunderstanding and (in some cases) derision that have accompanied it. Rather than being celebrated as an artistic polymath whose questioning of the fundamental tenets of Western art music led to a revolution in twentieth-century culture, Cage has often been characterized as, at best, a comedian and, at worst, a charlatan. Unable or unwilling to allow Cage and his work a fair hearing, or even to speak for themselves, musicians and commentators alike have frequently subverted his performances and misrepresented his ideas. To cite but two examples of such actions, in 1964 members of the New York Philharmonic Orchestra laughed, talked among themselves, played inappropriate material, and destroyed electronic equipment during performances of *Atlas Eclipticalis* (1962); and as recently as 1998, the philosopher Stan Godlovitch compared Cage's "silent" piece, *4' 33"*, to a nonexistent doughnut, served in an empty folded napkin with fresh coffee.

Yet Cage has had a profound—and essentially positive—influence on contemporary culture. His pioneering work with percussion, with the prepared piano, and with electronics was pivotal in opening music to new timbral possibilities; his advocacy of chance, indeterminacy, and alternative notational practices contributed significantly to what one of his teachers, Henry Cowell (1897–1965), characterized as "getting rid of the glue"; and his use of extant musics—usually in decontextualized form—preempted one of the principal preoccupations of postmodernism. Cage was instrumental in the creation of happenings and multimedia events and contributed significantly to the developing relationship between music and dance. His ultimate, and unprecedented, goal—as defined in *Silence* (1961), his first and best-known collection of writings—was "giving up control so that sounds can be sounds." And beyond this, Cage's three hundred-or-so compositions are complemented by an impressive body of prose and poetry, as well as considerable activity in the areas of performance and visual art. With the possible exception of Andy Warhol (1928?–87), no American artist working in a field other than popular music has had such an enormous impact on global culture.

This book's principal purpose is to present John Cage and his work from a sympathetic (though still hopefully objective) viewpoint, so that general readers, students, performers, music lovers, and others who are unfamiliar with his oeuvre can make up their *own* minds as to its value. Throughout, Cage's artistic achievements will be placed in their historical, environmental, intellectual, philosophical, and aesthetic contexts, so that they can be evaluated in relation to the society from which they emerged. His creative influence will be examined from the perspective of his contemporaries and successors; and his continuing legacy, as an artist and a thinker, will be considered in relation to present-day pluralism.

| | |

A number of people and institutions have contributed in important ways to the appearance of this volume. First and foremost is Judith McCulloh at the University of Illinois Press, who encouraged me to undertake its writing and then waited very patiently for its delivery. Laura Kuhn, of the John Cage Trust, was extremely helpful in selecting many of the photographs reproduced here, as were John Mazarak and David Patterson. Fiona Flower of Peters Edition in London was, as ever, efficient in handling requests—and not only regarding copyright permissions—relating to Cage's music. And Charles C. Cage, the fourth cousin once removed of John Cage, afforded invaluable help with the genealogical information that appears at the start of chapter 1. The University of Southampton provided me with research leave and support, not least during the academic year 2003–4, when much of this book was written.

Inevitably, I have relied on a number of extant sources for biographical and related information, including my own earlier writings, which—as an inveterate recycler—I have plundered heavily. These are *American Experimental Music, 1890–1940* (1990); the chapter on "Avant-Garde and Experimental Music" in *The Cambridge History of American Music* (1998); two chapters in *The Cambridge Companion to John Cage* (2002); and a contribution to Steven Johnson's *The New York Schools of Music and Visual Arts* (2002). Principal among the sources written by others are David Revill's *The Roaring Silence: John Cage, a Life* (1992) and the Cage chapter in Calvin Tomkins's *The Bride and the Bachelors* (1976). Also invaluable was James Pritchett's masterly study of *The Music of John Cage* (1993). On the one occasion I met Richard Kostelanetz, I mentioned to him that my copy of his *John Cage* (1971)—quite possibly the first book on American music that I ever bought—had seen so much use that it had literally fallen apart. Fortunately, Kostelanetz's *Conversing with Cage*, at least in its second edition (2003), has been spared this fate (so far . . . though the first edition is looking decidedly distressed). I have also benefited hugely over the last decade from the writings of and extended conversations with other Cage scholars, notably David Bernstein, William Brooks, David Patterson, Christopher Shultis, and especially Leta Miller.

Finally, my wife, Tamar, and children, Ben and Daisy, have—as ever—been supportive and ungrudging of the many hours I have spent with this project, rather than in family activities. It is therefore to them, and to my parents, that

4 the book is dedicated, in the hope that they—as much as its other readers—will come to understand what it is that makes John Cage such an important figure in American culture, and why it is that I have spent the last thirty-or-so years in admiration and awe of his achievements.

1 | The West Coast, 1912–42

JOHN MILTON CAGE JR. was born in Los Angeles on September 5, 1912. His parents were John Milton Cage Sr. (1886–1964) and Lucretia ("Crete") Harvey (1885–1969). Bald as these facts may be, they help us in several ways to understand the origins of Cage's unique persona. For, nature notwithstanding—Cage being gifted intellectually and musically from his earliest years—it was clearly nurture that had the more profound part to play in his development.

Genealogy

It is important to state at the outset that while Cage's voluminous writings and numerous interviews provide many details concerning his background, life, developing aesthetic views, and so on, his recollections were on occasion selective and sometimes suspiciously self-serving. His statements need, wherever possible, to be balanced by incontestable facts. Cage himself, in a 1981 letter to me, conceded, "I am a very poor historian." Thus, as R. F. Arragon implies in the quotation included in the colophon to this book, history is invented. This book is therefore as much an invention of history as are Cage's anecdotes, or even the facts that support or contest his memory.

That said, the extant material concerning Cage's genealogy—while tending to focus on his male antecedents—is still useful in establishing a genetic background that emphasizes idiosyncrasy over ordinariness. Moreover, Cage's ancestry—in stark contrast to that of at least two of his major composer contemporaries, Aaron Copland (1900–90) and George Gershwin (1898–1937)—firmly locates him as of native, rather than recently immigrated, American stock. Although ultimately of British descent, Cage's forebears had arrived in the New World in the early seventeenth century. The first American Cage—also named John—was a servant indentured to Thomas Cornwallis, who landed in St. Mary's County, Maryland, in 1623. Allegedly, a later "John Cage . . . helped Washington in the surveying of Virginia," though this statement is difficult to square with the information contained in the Cage Family Web Site.[1] Later Cages—notably Major William Cage (ca. 1745–1811)—moved further inland, to the western side of the Appalachians: the family name (and a family cemetery) can still be found at Cage's Bend in Sumner County, Tennessee. A number of the Tennessee Cages were active as Methodist preachers: for instance, Gustavus Adolphus Williamson Cage I (1819–1905), a grandson of Major William, was a Tennessee farmer who before the Civil War preached to both blacks and whites; he subsequently moved to Colorado. One of his children, Gustavus Adolphus Williamson Cage II (John Cage's grandfather), followed him into the Methodist Episcopalian church, traveling to Utah to decry Mormonism and to Wyoming to serve as a missionary.[2] John Cage's father was born in Colorado. Due perhaps to the "extraordinary puritanical righteousness" and temper of Gustavus Adolphus Williamson II, John Milton Sr. often ran away from home.[3]

Less is known of Crete Harvey's ancestry. She was born in Iowa to James Carey and Minnie Harvey, had a brother and four sisters, and due to her family's suspicion of knowledge had, as a child, needed to hide books in her bedroom. Prior to meeting John Cage Sr., Crete had apparently been married twice (though she was reportedly, and rather unbelievably, unable to remember her first husband's name). She was the pianist at the First Methodist Episcopalian church in Denver where Gustavus Cage was the preacher. Prior to the birth of John Jr., her marriage to John Sr. had resulted in two unsuccessful pregnancies: Gustavus Adolphus Williamson III was stillborn, and Gustavus Adolphus Williamson IV lived for only two weeks.

The potentially significant character traits that emerge from this genealogy include a certain pioneer spirit; doggedness in the pursuit of unpromising quarry; religious (or, better, quasi-religious) zeal; intense self-belief; musicality; eccentricity; and—due to the Cage family's long-established American roots—no sense

John Cage with his father, John Milton Cage Sr., and his grand-father, Gustavus Adolphus Williamson Cage II, ca. 1916, Denver, Colorado. Photographer unknown. Used by permission of the John Cage Trust.

of the pressure felt by recent immigrants to assimilate or conform. All of these traits came in one way or another to typify John Milton Cage Jr. as his personality formed during the West Coast years.

Growing Up

Notwithstanding the above comments relating to the nature half of the developmental equation, a number of major factors on the nurture side served to disrupt Cage's childhood and certainly impacted on his character. Foremost among these was his parents' relationship. Whether it was intrinsically unstable is difficult to determine, but the particular circumstances under which it operated are not. Just as Gustavus Adolphus Williamson had made concrete his father's religious interests by becoming a professional preacher, so did John Sr. take up Gustavus's penchant for invention. Gustavus, in 1909, had patented a device to facilitate use

"*My mother (Lucretia Harvey) Crete Cage*" *(ca. 1925). Photographer unknown. Used by permission of the John Cage Trust.*

of the typewriter; John Sr. spent his life imagining and creating in a manner that sometimes inclined more to the idealistic than the pragmatic.

The best known of John Sr.'s inventions was a gasoline-powered submarine that—rather unfortunately—gave off bubbles. It set "the world's record for staying underwater . . . by making an experimental trip on Friday the thirteenth [of September, or possibly December, 1912], with a crew of thirteen, staying underwater for thirteen hours."[4] Other submarine-related inventions included steering and propulsion systems and detection devices. John Sr. was also responsible for an AC-powered radio, a treatment for the common cold, airplane designs, and modifications to the internal combustion engine. However, some of these projects were less financially successful than others, leading to dramatic variations in family income and, by extension, residence: the bubble-blowing submarine bankrupted him, forcing the family's relocation, in 1915, to Michigan. By the time he was twelve, John Jr. had already lived in California (six or more locations in greater Los Angeles), Michigan (Ann Arbor and Detroit), and Ontario, Canada.

Crete, meanwhile, combined socializing with secretarial work. A member of various women's clubs in Michigan and California, she also worked as a journalist, latterly for the *Los Angeles Times*.[5] But the effects of her involuntary itinerancy—first on her relationship with John Sr., second on her son—were predictable. Cage described his parents' marriage as a "good one between bad people," but the anecdotal evidence suggests that a reversal of the adjectives might be equally appropriate.[6] Cage variously spoke of his mother as "never happy" and as someone who "never enjoyed having a good time." Periodically, like John Sr. in his childhood, Crete would run away, "saying she was never coming back." Cage's father would then have to assure John Jr. that she would indeed return.[7] On one occasion, Cage overheard his father saying to Crete, "Get ready: we're going to New Zealand Saturday." Cage prepared himself, reading everything about New Zealand that he could find in the school library. "Saturday came. Nothing happened. The project was not even mentioned."[8] Finally, it is clear that John Sr. saw himself as henpecked: he worked mostly from home, and Crete kept him busy running errands. Once, when Cage was arguing with his mother, John Sr.'s telling response was, "Son John, your mother is always right, even when she's wrong."[9]

Apart from the frequent changes of domicile and the instability of his parents' marriage, Cage must also have been affected by the presence in the family home of several of Crete's relatives. His maternal grandmother (Minnie Harvey) possessed a religious zeal comparable to that of his paternal grandfather. One day, as Cage tiptoed across the living room to retrieve a manuscript, she awoke and addressed him sharply: "John, are you ready for the second coming of the Lord?"[10] Two of Crete's sisters, Marge and Phoebe, contributed to the musical environment in which Cage grew up. Marge was a contralto who sang at the family church; Cage loved to hear her voice. Phoebe, meanwhile, was one of his earliest piano teachers after he had commenced lessons in the fourth grade. Devoted to the music of the late nineteenth century, and rather disinterested in the work of Bach and Beethoven, she seems to have encouraged Cage's early obsession with the music of Edvard Grieg. In terms of his practice regime, Cage was "more interested in sight-reading than in running up and down the scales. Being a virtuoso didn't interest me at all."[11]

Cage was clearly a precocious child, both musically and academically. At age five, he was taken by his mother to a symphony concert where he apparently stood in the aisle, enraptured, for two hours. Later, when his parents acceded to his wish to study the piano, he remembered playing the baby grand they had bought while it was being moved into the family home. Later still, he spent many hours browsing through the music shelves at Los Angeles Public Library.[12] Academically, he achieved top grades for his elementary school work in Michigan and California; this pattern lasted through high school. However, Cage was a self-described "sissy," which led to much bullying: "[T]hey made fun of me at every opportunity . . . if I read one of the papers I had written they would simply respond by laughing. . . . People would lie in wait for me and beat me up and I never would defend myself because I had gone to Sunday school and they had said to turn the other cheek, which I took seriously."[13]

Unsurprisingly, given these experiences and the frequent family relocations, Cage's anecdotes concerning his childhood tend to focus on his out-of-school activities, family reminiscences, or topics of pleasure or success. We hear almost nothing of boyhood friends, and the general impression is of a lonely only child, forced back on his inner resources, trying to avoid the tensions of his home, and of necessity self-reliant. Once returned to Los Angeles, he spent much time apparently on his own, exploring the neighborhood or playing unsupervised at the beach. A notable, but singular, exception to this solitary existence is found in stories concerning his membership in the Boy Scouts. In his teens, he persuaded a Los Angeles radio station, KNX, to broadcast a weekly Scout program. Cage was the compère and principal performer; other parts of the hour-long show, which ran for around two years, were provided by other Scouts—who sang, played instruments, and spoke of their scouting experiences—and by members of the clergy.

By the time he attended Los Angeles High School (1923–28), Cage's life was more settled. Family finances were less volatile (though it is uncertain whether the same could be said of his parents' relationship), and consequently there were fewer changes of address. Furthermore, the bullying had stopped. Although he failed to get into the school's Glee Club, his piano skills developed apace under the tuition of Fannie Charles Dillon. His academic work also continued to flourish, and he excelled in French, classical languages, and oratory. His senior year at high school saw him achieve much: he was contributing editor of the school's monthly French-language newspaper, *Le Flambeau*; at the Hollywood Bowl he represented the school in the Southern California Oratorical Contest, with a speech entitled "Other People Think," and won first prize; his teachers elected him to an elite group of "Ephebians," citing his "scholarship, leadership, and character"; he was appointed class valedictorian; and he graduated with the highest scholastic average in the school's history.[14]

Cage even made some friends, though one facet of these friendships is significant. Kimmis Hendrick was a Christian Scientist and Hugh Nibley a Mormon, and the three adolescents engaged in frequent theological debate. Cage had decided to follow Gustavus Adolphus Williamson into ministry with the First Methodist Episcopalian church, but in his final high school year he became heavily involved with the Liberal Catholic church. His parents were appalled and issued the ultimatum that he must choose between them and his newfound religion. In retrospect, what occurred next was a pivotal moment: having decided—like James and John when they left their father Zebedee—to accept Jesus's call to follow him, Cage was persuaded by the Liberal Catholic priest, the Reverend Tettemer, to go home: "There are many religions [but] you have only one mother and father."[15]

Cage's next calling was to Pomona College in Claremont, California, a New England–style private institution, which he entered in September 1928. During the course of his two years there he lost religion and discovered the arts, helping to organize an exhibition of modern paintings, writing a short story that was published in the Pomona literary magazine, winning an English prize, and being exposed to Beethoven and other previously taboo composers via a friend's record collection. Academically, though, Cage's promise was not fulfilled in conventional terms. During his sophomore year his grades took a dive as he became disenchanted with the norms of pedagogy, choosing instead to answer assignments in the style of Gertrude Stein. His end-of-year report noted, "Does not plan to return. Going to travel in Europe." Cage had persuaded his parents that his educational interests would be served best by dropping out of college and pursuing independent study abroad.[16]

Independence

In the late spring of 1930, Cage hitchhiked to Galveston, Texas, and boarded a ship bound for Le Havre, embarking on a voyage of discovery both literal and metaphorical. In literal terms, his journey to and through Europe was similar to that undertaken by countless other New World youngsters intent on exploring the Old World. His eighteen-month sojourn—spent principally in Paris, but also apparently taking in Berlin, Capri, Dessau, Madrid, Mallorca, Seville, and Algeria—brought him into contact with sights, sounds, and smells very different from those of California. He also inevitably encountered civilizations and societies founded on principles other than commerce and capitalism. Cage's voyage of discovery continued long after his return to the United States, however. During the remainder of the decade, he met major challenges and choices concerning his artistic vocation, his musical aesthetics, and his sexuality.

Cage's initial destination, Paris, "enchanted but rather overwhelmed the seventeen-year-old."[17] It also resulted in the first of Cage's obsessions (later examples include mycology and houseplants): he spent a number of weeks ensconced in the Bibliothèque Mazarine (part of the Institut de France, located on the Quai de Conti) studying the balustrades of fifteenth-century Gothic architecture. The many hours spent in the library were supplemented by field trips to the cathedrals of Notre Dame, Chartres, and Beauvais.[18] Cage's studies were brought to an abrupt halt by an encounter—presumably during the summer vacation period—with a Pomona professor, José Pijoan. On hearing of his former pupil's current occupation, Pijoan gave Cage "a violent kick in the pants" and arranged for him to work at the studio of the modernist architect Arno Goldfinger.[19] Cage's tasks there included "measuring the dimensions of rooms which [Goldfinger] was set to modernize, answering the telephone, and drawing Greek columns."[20] After several months, though, Cage left the firm, having overheard Goldfinger saying that the profession of architect required a complete commitment to architecture. This was something Cage was unwilling to do.

At this stage, Cage seemed unsure of his future vocation, other than that it would be artistic. He was equally interested in music, poetry, and art and tried his hand at all three during the following months. In retrospect, we can see here the first blossoming of Cage's post-1950 creative polymathy, but at the time its principal musical manifestations included a brief period of piano tuition with Lazare Lévy of the Paris Conservatoire, further encounters with "taboo" music by Bach and Mozart, and the discovery (instigated via his attendance at a concert by John Kirkpatrick) of contemporary works by Paul Hindemith, Aleksandr Skryabin, and Igor Stravinsky. Later, in Berlin, he attended a concert that concluded with works by Hindemith and Ernst Toch that had been specifically written for phonograph records.[21] While visiting Mallorca, Cage made his own first attempts at composition, using a complex mathematical process to ape Bach. But "the results were so unmusical, from my then point of view, that I threw them away."[22]

Having discovered girls in high school, in Paris Cage discovered boys. His first, brief, affair was with John Goheen, the son of a music professor at Queen's College. Subsequently, and more lastingly, he teamed up with Don Sample, with whom—at Pomona—he had organized an exhibition of modern paintings.[23] Cage and Sample traveled together through Europe, and Cage learned much concerning the arts from his older companion. In the fall of 1931 they returned to America via Cuba and drove to Los Angeles in a Model-T Ford.

Among the souvenirs taken back to California was a Bauhaus catalog. Although the majority of Cage's time in Europe had been spent in France, the greater cultural influences on him were German. While in Paris, Cage and Sample may have attended an exhibition at the Société des Artistes Décorateurs Français, the German section of which was designed by the Bauhaus members Walter Gropius, László Moholy-Nagy, Herbert Bayer, and Marcel Breuer; records at the Dessau Bauhaus note Cage's and Sample's visit there. And Harry Hay (an actor, early gay activist, and a friend of Cage's from Los Angeles High School) sang some of Cage's early songs around this time, which were staged "in the Bauhaus style, including the costumes."[24] Further Bauhaus connections were established through one of Cage's and Sample's early residences, the guest apartment at the King's Road house of the architect Rudolph Schindler. It was there that Cage probably met Galka Scheyer, a Bauhaus devotee who was also the U.S. representative for the "Blue Four"—Lyonel Feininger, Alexey von Jawlensky, Paul Klee, and Wassily Kandinsky. Scheyer lent Cage some of Klee's paintings and introduced him to Walter Arensberg and the architect Richard Neutra.

Cage's relationship with Sample now became promiscuous, with both men indulging freely in other liaisons.[25] Cage also became involved in an affair with Rudolph Schindler's ex-wife, Pauline, who was fifteen years older than him and lived at Ojai, some distance to the north of Los Angeles. It is worth noting at this juncture that many of Cage's scores include the date and location at which they were completed, a useful aid in plotting his movements. Thus the manuscript of one of his earliest works, the *Composition for Three Voices*, is inscribed "Ojai 1934" and dedicated to Pauline Schindler. Another early dedicatee was Richard Buhlig. After returning from Europe, Cage had continued composing, though his compositional method now consisted of "[improvising] at the piano and then [trying] to write [the notes] down quickly before they got away."[26] Most of these pieces were vocal, and Cage's catalog of extant works details settings of Aeschylus (1932) and Gertrude Stein (1933). There were also, apparently, other (lost) pieces using writings from the magazine *transition* (to which he had been introduced by Sample) and Ecclesiastes.

Although Cage would eventually study composition with Buhlig, his initial contact with him had a different purpose. Despite the relative economic health of California during the 1920s, by 1933 the effects of the Great Depression were cutting deep into society.[27] Cage's parents had had to move to an apartment, and Cage himself—after various cohabitations with Don Sample—was forced into taking a job as a gardener at a Santa Monica auto court, "working in return for an apartment and a large room over the garage."[28] Capitalizing on his enthusiasm for modern painting and music, Cage showed remarkable initiative and self-motivation in raising funds by organizing lectures, delivered to local housewives at a rate of $2.50 for a series of ten one-hour sessions. Initially, all went well. Perhaps as a result of his solitary childhood, Cage was a gifted researcher: each week, he investigated the current topic at the Los Angeles Public Library and then delivered his findings to the assembled housewives. However, when the time came to talk on Arnold Schoenberg (1874–1951), in whose work he had become increasingly interested, Cage was stumped. He could not obtain any recordings; and apart from one movement from Schoenberg's opus 25 *Suite for Piano*, he could not perform any of the music, finding it too difficult to play.[29]

About a year earlier, Cage had decided, on a whim, to contact Richard Buhlig, who had given the American premiere of Schoenberg's opus 11 piano pieces, and whom Cage somewhat illogically decided must be living in Los Angeles. Remarkably, this turned out to be correct. When Cage asked if he could hear him play the Schoenberg pieces, Buhlig refused and hung up. When the time came for Cage's lecture on Schoenberg, he contacted Buhlig again, this time waiting outside his house until he came home. Buhlig once more refused to perform for Cage's lecture but offered to look at his compositions.[30] As a result, Cage came to learn much from Buhlig concerning time and structure, was introduced to another student—Grete Sultan—with whom he would collaborate in later life, and worked his way through Ebenezer Prout's famous textbooks on *Harmony* and *Musical Form*.[31] Buhlig's reward was to become the dedicatee of Cage's *Sonata for Two Voices*, written in Santa Monica in 1933.

It was through Buhlig—whom he described as "a wonderful, cultivated man, [who] taught me a great deal"—that Cage met Henry Cowell.[32] Cowell, by now in his mid-thirties, had already developed a reputation throughout America and Europe for his self-styled ultramodernism. By 1933, he had written nearly five hundred pieces (though many of these were either juvenilia or inconsequentially short), plus the remarkable book *New Musical Resources;* had given numerous concerts of his own music throughout the Northern Hemisphere; had been the first American composer to visit the Soviet Union; was founding editor of *New Music Edition;* and had become—as Cage later put it—"the open sesame for new music in America."[33] Cowell had also, principally through the New Music Society of California and Varèse's Pan American Association of Composers, promoted many concerts of contemporary music, including one in Paris—ironically given shortly after Cage had left the city—featuring pieces by Charles Ives, Carl Ruggles, Adolph Weiss, and Cowell himself.

Buhlig had suggested to Cage that he send some of his work to Cowell, in the hope that it might be published in *New Music*. Cowell's response was to invite Cage to have his *Sonata for Clarinet* (September 1933, San Francisco) performed at a New Music Society workshop in San Francisco. Cage hitchhiked up the coast only to find, on his arrival, that the chosen clarinetist had, after taking one look at the piece on the day of the performance, decided it was too difficult to play. Cage was required to perform the work himself on the piano. As Calvin Tomkins notes, "[T]he incident had a bearing on [Cage's] subsequent decision not to rely on conventional musicians."[34] However, Cage and his work intrigued

Cowell, who supposedly taught him "'dissonant counterpoint and composition . . . for a season in California'"[35] and encouraged him to study with Schoenberg, whom Cowell considered the greatest living composer, and to whom Cage had already been drawn aesthetically.

Cage's works of this period—the *Sonata for Clarinet, Sonata for Two Voices, Composition for Three Voices,* and the pedantically titled *Solo with Obbligato Accompaniment of Two Voices in Canon, and Six Short Inventions on the Subject of the Solo* (Carmel, 1933–34)—are all redolent to some extent of Schoenberg's "method of composing with twelve tones which are related only with one another" (or serialism, as it is more commonly known). In Schoenberg's original formulation, a single ordering (or row) of the twelve notes of the chromatic scale—along with its inversion, retrograde, retrograde-inversion, and the transpositions of these variants—supplied all of the pitch material for a given work. The middle movement of Cage's *Sonata for Clarinet* follows this plan quite simply in employing the prime (basic) form of the row, together with its transposed inversion, retrograde, retrograde-inversion, and fragments of these variants.[36] The outer movements of the sonata are more freely chromatic, though the last is a rhythmically varied retrograde of the first. In the three slightly later pieces, Cage developed his own version of serialism by avoiding pitch repetitions in a given twenty-five-pitch (two-octave) range, in which the middle octave is usually shared by the voices; the counterpoint is accordingly freer, though palindromes and other learned devices are still much in evidence.[37] In this twenty-five-pitch serialism can be detected the possible influence of Buhlig and of Cowell's dissonant counterpoint, a method of composition (which emphasized dissonance rather than consonance) devised by Charles Seeger initially in conjunction with his own teaching of Cowell at Berkeley in the mid-1910s.[38]

Such musical developments notwithstanding, however, Cage was as prone as any other citizen to the effects of the Depression. As he put it some years later, "I had no job. No one could get work."[39] Accordingly, he was to be found during the remainder of 1933 and the early part of 1934 engaged in a number of menial tasks: he carried out research for his father and others; he worked at the Blue Bird Tearooms on Ocean Avenue, Carmel, where—in foraging for wild strawberries to supplement his diet—he first discovered the joys of mycology; and he served in the nonprofit arts-and-crafts shop that his mother had established.[40] As a result of this last job, he met Xenia Andreevna Kashevaroff (1913–95), one of the six daughters of a Russian Orthodox priest from Juneau, Alaska. Xenia was a student at Reed College who had wandered into Crete's shop. Cage's response was definitive: "It was love at first sight on my part, not on hers . . . the moment I saw her I was convinced that we were going to be married."[41] A few weeks later, on Xenia's next visit to the shop, Cage invited her to dine with him, and at that dinner proposed: "She was put off a little bit. She said she'd have to think about it."[42]

Xenia had plenty of time to consider Cage's proposal. Although he continued to paint, his compositions were attracting the greater interest. Following Cowell's suggestion that he should have lessons with Schoenberg, Cage arranged to undertake preliminary instruction, in New York, with Adolph Weiss (1891–1971), the first American to have studied with Schoenberg.[43] Cage hitchhiked to New York in the late spring of 1934 and stayed for approximately eight months. His daily routine was demanding: rising at 4 A.M., he would spend four hours in preparation for the day's session with Weiss. He then traveled to Brooklyn, where, despite the degradations of the Depression, he had been fortunate in obtaining a job washing walls at the YWCA. On his return to Manhattan he would have a meal, take his lesson with Weiss, and then until midnight play bridge with the Weisses, with or without Cowell or Wallingford Reigger. Apart from his formal studies, which have been documented by Michael Hicks, Cage also learned something else from Weiss, albeit indirectly: "One of the things that impressed me when I worked with [him] was that he had written a large amount of music and almost none of it was played. He was somewhat embittered because of this, and I determined then and there that if I did get to the point of writing music I would consider my responsibility only half finished if I didn't get it performed."[44]

In addition to his lessons with Weiss, Cage was also awarded a scholarship to attend Cowell's courses at the New School for Social Research.[45] This exempted him from paying fees, and he was thus able to experience firsthand Cowell's highly innovative teaching of world musics and other topics. Cage undoubtedly met some of the Cowell circle—including Henry Brant, Ruth Crawford, Harry Partch, William Russell, Carl Ruggles, Charles Seeger, and Edgard Varèse, all of whom were in New York around this time—and would have been exposed to the current publications of *New Music Quarterly* and its associated record label, including music by Crawford, Charles Ives, Dane Rudhyar, Ruggles, Varèse, and Weiss. Cage tacitly acknowledges these and other influences in his 1959 essay "History of Experimental Music in the United States."[46] More generally, Cage would also have benefited from New York's extraordinary musical life and the possibilities it created for young composers. As Carol J. Oja has written, "New York City placed [them] at an auspicious cultural crossroads. There they could stand, with all their belongings in one suitcase, free to roam in whatever direction their imaginations might lead."[47]

Toward the end of December 1934, Cage and Cowell drove back to California. By this time, Schoenberg, who first arrived on America's East Coast in October

1933, had for health reasons decamped to Hollywood. Cage joined his classes in January 1935.[48] Although some authors have suggested that Cage embellished, or even fabricated, the details of his relationship with Schoenberg, Michael Hicks has proved conclusively that Cage studied with the sexagenarian Viennese master for around eighteen months, taking classes in analysis, counterpoint, harmony, and composition at the University of Southern California and the University of California at Los Angeles. As with the Cowell courses at the New School, Cage was able to take Schoenberg's classes mostly without payment. Although he supposedly needed the income, Schoenberg often taught his students *gratis*, as he believed, somewhat immodestly, that "it will damage them less to study with me than with a poorer teacher."[49] However, despite his later statements suggesting otherwise, Cage found the experience of studying with Schoenberg somewhat dispiriting, as his extant letters to Weiss confirm. Schoenberg's general attitude toward his pupils, from Berg through Webern to Cage, was dismissive: indeed, he told one USC class that his aim was "'to make it impossible for you to write music.'"[50]

The Cagean literature contains numerous anecdotes concerning Schoenberg, most of which appear to be based in truth. Cage's free tuition, for instance, is explained thus: "He said, 'You probably can't afford my price,' and I said, 'You don't need to mention it because I don't have any money.' So he said, 'Will you devote your life to music?' and I said I would."[51] In some secondary sources, as well as Cage's 1989 "Autobiographical Statement," this story concludes with Schoenberg adding, "'In that case, I will teach you free of charge.'"[52] Class events are recalled in a number of Cage's collections of writings and conversations. For instance, *Silence* contains pertinent reminiscences, and in *For the Birds*, Cage and Daniel Charles discuss Schoenberg on several occasions.[53] Yet despite the fact that Cage "worshipped Schoenberg—I saw in him an extraordinary musical mind, one that was greater and more perceptive than the others," he ultimately parted company with him over the issue of harmony, for which Cage believed himself to have no feeling.[54] Schoenberg explained that Cage would, as a consequence of this, "always encounter an obstacle, that it would be as though I came to a wall through which I could not pass. I said, 'In that case I will devote my life to beating my head against that wall.'"[55]

Given the subsequent direction of Cage's work, it is worth stepping aside briefly to consider the legacy of his different experiences of learning with Schoenberg and Cowell. Although it was Cowell, the ardent admirer of Schoenberg, who first recommended that Cage study with him, in reality the two older composers were worlds apart in terms of their basic musical aesthetics. Schoenberg, in his work and in his teaching, was fundamentally attached to the Austro-German musical tradition, and he believed that his pupils should learn by the same methods he had employed, autodidactically, in his youth: by imitation of past masters. Schoenberg taught Cage that structure and discipline are absolutely necessary in musical composition; the difficulty lay in Schoenberg's insistence that that structure and discipline should be based in harmonic considerations. Cowell, in stark contrast, was a musical naif who knew as much about Appalachian, Irish, Chinese, Japanese, and Tahitian music as he did about Western art music. To him, all sounds were potentially musical and as such could be brought together freely in a composition. Notwithstanding the intricacies of musical theory expounded and exhibited in *New Musical Resources* and elsewhere, Cowell was at root a free spirit, someone who—unlike Cage at this stage in his life—was "not attached to what seemed to so many to be the important question: whether to follow Schoenberg or Stravinsky."[56] The rapprochement forged by Cage between the polarized and equally paradigmatic aesthetic influences of Schoenberg and Cowell was to define his subsequent life's work.

Early Career

Concurrently with his Schoenbergian studies at USC and UCLA, Cage was developing a nascent career as a professional musician. He and Xenia Andreevna Kashevaroff married in Yuma, Arizona, on June 7, 1935. Initially, they lived with Cage's parents, but the desire for a home of their own, as well as the need to generate family income, led Cage to take on a number of mainly music-related jobs.

Cage's compositions of this time continued along previously established lines, though with the twenty-five-note serialism replaced by a method in which the whole (twelve-note) row was never used in its entirety. Rather, the row's intervals were used to generate motivic segments; connections between these segments were made by "referring to the final note of each segment and its position within the row."[57] The pieces using this technique include the *Two Pieces for Piano* (1935), *Three Pieces for Flute Duet* (1935), *Metamorphosis* for piano (1938), *Five Songs* (to texts by e.e. cummings, whom Cage met through Galka Scheyer; 1938), and *Music for Wind Instruments* (1938). Apart from their common compositional method, these works also share several other features: each has at least two movements; much of the writing is by nature somewhat pithy; there is—as one might expect—little sense of traditional harmony in evidence; repetition is invariably preferred over variation; and the overall effect is not dissimilar to that of the *Three Stein Songs* of 1933. Furthermore, the quasi-modality and occasional lyricism of the Stein songs also resurface in some of the cummings settings and in the slower movements of *Metamorphosis* and *Music for Wind Instruments*. Indeed, the trajectory suggested by these works is not hugely dissimilar to that of Erik Satie (1866–1925), Virgil Thomson (1896–1989), or the Copland of *Grohg* (1922–25) and the *Piano Variations* (1930). There is nothing here that prepares one for the impact of Cage's better-known later music.

However, contemporaneously to these "traditional" pieces, Cage was also writing music that smacked more of the future. First, the short piano piece *Quest* (1935)—which was written for dance accompaniment—demonstrates his early interest in investigating collaborative media as well as his willingness to adapt his music to the demands of performance. Harmonic writing and carefully placed dynamics are much in evidence here. Second, in two other works from 1935–36, he abandons intervals in favor of noises, specifically those of percussion instruments.

In the summer of 1933, Cage had been much impressed by a Hollywood Bowl performance of Varèse's percussion piece *Ionisation* (1931). Subsequently, he would surely have been aware of the emerging repertoire for the ensemble, not least via Cowell's *New Music Edition* (which, among other relevant items, published *Ionisation* in 1934 and an all-percussion issue in 1936). And he may also, even at this early date, have known Cowell's own percussion piece *Ostinato Pianissimo* (1934), which was eventually premiered by Cage's group in 1943. Cage was already, in his classes with Schoenberg, discovering his inability to work with traditional pitch material (such as harmony) and must therefore have been interested in the possibilities afforded by unpitched music. As he explicitly stated at a later date, while sound possesses four characteristics—frequency, duration, amplitude, and timbre—only duration is common not only to pitched and unpitched sounds but also to the silence that lies between them.[58]

Finally, in 1935 or thereabouts, a short-term job brought Cage into contact with the experimental filmmaker Oskar Fischinger.[59] Fischinger suggested to Cage that there is a "spirit which is inside each of the objects of this world . . . all we need to do to liberate that spirit is to brush past the object and to draw forth its sound. [Subsequently] I never stopped touching things, making them sound and resound, to discover what sounds they could produce."[60] Perhaps it was just such an interest that inspired the *Quartet* (1935): although written in four extended movements and lasting around twenty minutes, the score contains no instrumental specifications. Indeed, given that Cage once remarked that his intention—at Galka Scheyer's suggestion—had been to "write some music that [Fischinger] would use to make an abstract film," it is conceivable that the *Quartet* is actually the soundtrack to one of Fischinger's works.[61] A second percussion

19

piece, the three-movement *Trio* (1936), uses such specified instruments as wood-blocks, tom-toms, bamboo sticks, and bass drums and is in many ways redolent of the *Three Dance Movements* by William Russell (1905–92), which had appeared in the *New Music* percussion issue.

The Cages' accommodation problems were solved temporarily through Xenia becoming an apprentice to the bookbinder Hazel Dreis. Dreis required her apprentices to live in her large Santa Monica house, and as a result of his residency there Cage developed skills as a designer and—by virtue of "borrowing" the apprentices each evening—was able to form his first percussion group. It performed on kitchen utensils, bookbinding equipment, and objects salvaged from scrap yards and gave informal concerts—though Cage was never able to interest Schoenberg in attending one.[62] Xenia's apprenticeship apparently carried no stipend, but Cage was able to generate income (not for the last time) by carrying out research assignments, in this instance for law firms. However, as he noted later, "[E]veryone was as poor as a church mouse."[63] In 1937, Cage became an assistant at the UCLA elementary school and a staff member of the Westwood Training School; he acted as an accompanist, gave classes in percussion, and continued further his collaborations with dancers as accompanist for technical classes and as composer for actual dance works. Among the concrete benefits of these activities were the development of musical structures based on the "counts" of the dancers and—when requested to write a piece for the annual water ballet performed by the UCLA swimming team—the water gong. The swimmers found it difficult to hear music while they were submerged; but when a vibrating gong was lowered into the water, they were better able to keep time. Cage later employed the sliding tone effects produced by moving the gong in and out of water in his concert works.

Later in the academic year, in the spring of 1938, Cage collaborated with his Aunt Phoebe in a UCLA extension course—Musical Accompaniments for Rhythmic Expression—that combined his interests in percussion and dance. Perhaps following Fischinger's suggestion, the class also experimented with unusual sound sources, and Cage was led to make his first investigations of the piano's innards.[64] However, none of these jobs promised permanence; moreover, John Jr. and Xenia may well have felt the need to escape from the potentially suffocating proximity of John Sr. and Crete. Cage's musical interests had never been entirely approved of—"The general feeling was that [a musician] wasn't a good thing to be"—and remnants of this attitude persisted through much of Cage's life.[65] Crete's damning critique of the 1935 *Quartet* is typical: "I enjoyed it, but where are you going to put it?"[66] Consequently, in the summer of 1938 the Cages determined to seek work in northern California. After traveling first to Carmel, where two of Xenia's sisters lived, Cage drove up to San Francisco to follow a lead suggested by Cowell. Although he was by this time approximately two years into a stint in San Quentin Penitentiary, as the result of being convicted on a morals charge, Cowell had continued to teach Lou Harrison (1917–2003). Harrison, like Cage, had benefited from studying with Cowell and Schoenberg and was similarly interested in percussion music and dance composition. As Cowell had suspected, the two young men immediately developed a bond and became lifelong friends. Through Harrison's numerous artistic contacts in the Bay Area and beyond, Cage was offered a position as an accompanist at the interdisciplinary Cornish School in Seattle. The two years he spent there were among the most formative and important of his life.[67]

Cage's immediate employer at the Cornish School was the dancer and choreographer Bonnie Bird, a former member of the Martha Graham Company. Apart from accompanying Bird's dance classes, Cage composed new works for specific (dance and concert) performances, gave talks, and continued to develop the percussion orchestra, initially by appropriating instruments belonging to Lore Deja, who had recently left Seattle. The new works were largely predicated in the resources available to Cage at the Cornish School. A percussion concert on December 9, 1938—the first of three given at Cornish by Cage during his time there—featured the existing *Quartet*. Exactly a year later, his second concert included the premiere of the *First Construction (in Metal)* (1939). In the interim, a dance program on March 24 and 25, 1939, afforded Cage the opportunity to compose scores for two items: he contributed several numbers to a revival of Jean Cocteau's *Marriage at the Eiffel Tower* (1939), his co-composers being Cowell and George McKay; and he utilized some of the Cornish radio school's electronic equipment in the *Imaginary Landscape No. 1* (1939). The "Cage Percussion Players" also gave concerts outside Seattle in California, Idaho, Montana, and Oregon—some of these events being promoted in association with Lou Harrison—and at Mills College, with artists from the Chicago School of Design. This brought Cage into contact with László Moholy-Nagy.

Cage seems to have relished the opportunity to talk publicly on general developments in contemporary music and on issues related more specifically to his own activities. For instance, on October 10, 1938, he addressed the Seattle chapter of Pro Musica, and on December 11 spoke on "New Directions in Music" at the first meeting of the newly formed Seattle Artists League. Most crucially, on February 18, 1940, a talk given to the Seattle Artists League titled "What Next in American Art?" formed the basis of what is in effect Cage's artistic manifesto,

Lou Harrison and John Cage (rear), Doris Dennison, Margaret Jansen, Xenia Cage (front), rehearsing for a concert at Mills College on July 17, 1940. Photographer unknown. Used by permission of the Oakland Tribune Collection, the Oakland Museum of California, Gift of the Alameda Newspaper Group.

the lecture published in 1958 as "The Future of Music: Credo."[68] The "Credo" is an extremely important document for three main reasons: it neatly summarizes Cage's contemporaneous concerns; it gives a remarkably accurate account of those issues that were to occupy him for much of the remainder of his artistic life; and it covertly acknowledges some of the principal influences on his developing musical and aesthetic viewpoint.

The "Credo" has three main foci:

> 1. The desire to use all available sounds in musical composition (with the implication that sounds should be allowed to be themselves, to paraphrase Cage) (lines 1–15, 46–48) and the citation of percussion music as an intermediate stage in this process (lines 68–71);

2. The anticipation of, and search for, electronic instruments and music (lines 16–45, 84–89);

3. The establishment of new methods of organizing sounds (lines 49–52, 58–67, 72–83, 90–91) and—by implication—the need for new notational systems to contain these methods (lines 53–57).[69]

In its typographical format, the "Credo" is almost identical to Luigi Russolo's *The Art of Noises* (1913) and other futurist manifestos such as Balilla Pratella's "Manifesto of Futurist Musicians" (1910), in which important remarks are rendered in capital letters. However, Cage differs from Russolo and Pratella in having the upper-case sections of text form a continuous line of thought. In addition, there are a number of specific correspondences of ideology and even phraseology between Cage and Russolo. Another, more recent, source of ideological and phraseological influence was Carlos Chávez's book *Toward a New Music* (1937), notably in relation to Cage's thoughts on timbral diversity, sound libraries, and the instruments of Lev Termen (Léon Thérémin). In more general ways, Cage's text demonstrates clear indebtedness to Cowell's *New Musical Resources* (1930) and also cribs from a program note Cowell provided for the Cornish concert on December 9, 1939, which employs the phrase "the future of music."[70] Finally, another major contemporary figure lurking in the background of the "Credo" is Varèse, notably in Cage's use of the characteristic term "organized sound."[71]

In its relationship with Cage's recent music, the lecture-manifesto most obviously evokes percussion pieces (including the *Quartet, Trio,* and *First Construction*), new acoustic and electronic sound sources (such as the string/prepared piano and the frequency recordings of *Imaginary Landscape No. 1*), innovative notational practices (nascently employed in the *Quartet* and the *Imaginary Landscape*), and especially new methods of organizing sounds. In *Music for Wind Instruments,* some movements of *Metamorphosis* and the *Five Songs,* and especially *Imaginary Landscape No. 1,* Cage had already created formal structures based on duration, using quasi-mathematical methods and apparently acknowledging, albeit tacitly, Cowell's example in the *United Quartet* (1936) and *Pulse* (1939). For instance, in the *Imaginary Landscape,* there are four large sections, each of fifteen 6/4 measures divided 5 : 5 : 5; each large section is succeeded by a contrasting shorter section in which the number of 6/4 measures increases arithmetically (1 : 2 : 3 : 4). Thus, in effect, the durational structure is precomposed and the music made to fit it.

With the *First Construction (in Metal),* Cage hit on a refinement of this procedure that served as the structural basis for almost all of his subsequent music through the early 1950s. In "square-root form," as it is usually called, a series of numbers denotes the macro- and the microcosmic proportions of a given piece. The essence of square-root form is that a durational unit of x measures is repeated x times, giving an overall length for the work of x^2 measures. In the case of the *First Construction*, the numerical series 4 : 3 : 2 : 3 : 4 (=16) outlines the number of units in each of the work's five main sections, as well as the relative phrase-lengths of each of the sixteen-measure sections constituting those units.[72] The supposed total length of the piece is therefore 16^2 (=256) measures of 4/4, though Cage somewhat illogically appends a nine-measure coda. A further benefit of durational structuring is that it invites the possibility of (simultaneous) co-composition. *Double Music* (April 1941) was written jointly by Cage and Harrison: of the work's four "voices," Cage wrote the first and third, Harrison the second and fourth. Beyond agreement on the tempo, meter, and overall length of the piece, the two composers operated separately in choosing different ways in which to subdivide its two hundred measures and different musical materials with which to fill those measures. Although never written, a *Triple Music*—with a third composer, Merton Brown—was also envisaged.

By the early 1940s, Cage's search for new timbral resources had generated copious results. In percussive terms, his own works employed a huge battery, ranging from the conventional (orchestral bells, cymbals, tam-tam, wood blocks, bass drum) through the exotic (oxen bells, Japanese temple gongs, teponaxtle, lion's roar, quijadas) to the distinctly unusual (graduated tin cans, brake drums, water gong, cricket callers, conch shell). There were even attempts to interact with the everyday: *Living Room Music* (1940) employs household objects such as newspapers and magazines, tables, books, and architectural elements including walls and door frames. It also, in its second movement, employs a speech quartet to declaim a text by Gertrude Stein in a manner obviously resembling that of Ernst Toch's *Geographical Fugue* (1930). Cage had heard an early version of this work in a concert in Berlin in 1930, and Toch had taught at two institutions—the New School for Social Research and USC—where Cage had studied.[73] On the proto-electronic front, the series of *Imaginary Landscape* pieces (*No. 1*, 1939; *Nos. 2* and *3*, 1942; their generic title is an acknowledgment of the influence of Paul Klee) had utilized variable-speed turntables and frequency recordings, an electronic buzzer and amplified radio aerial coil, an amplified marimbula, and a recording of a generator whine. These developments were also influenced by Cage's recollections of the 1930 Berlin concert and possibly by some of the theoretical writings that had preceded it.[74]

By far the most important innovation, however, had been Cage's development of the prepared piano, a grand piano that is timbrally altered through the insertion between its strings of metal, plastic, wooden, rubber, and other objects (typically screws, bolts with or without nuts, erasers, and weather stripping). Although the instrument made its formal debut in *Bacchanale* (1940), a dance score written to accompany choreography by one of Bonnie Bird's students, Syvilla Fort, it had experienced a long gestation.[75] Cage was well aware of Cowell's investigations of alternative piano timbres, such as keyboard clusters (for example, in *The Tides of Manaunaun* [ca. 1917] and *Dynamic Motion* [1916]) and the direct manipulation of the strings (for example, in *Aeolian Harp* [ca. 1923] and *The Banshee* [1925]). Cowell had also muted the piano strings manually (in *Ostinato Pianissimo* [1934]) and hit them directly with a timpani stick and with a metal object (in *A Composition* [1925]). In the 1938 UCLA extension course co-taught with his Aunt Phoebe, Cage had tied various objects to the strings of an upright piano;[76] and during one of Bird's dance classes, a metal rod rolling into the piano had given him further pause for thought.[77] This last incident presumably led to the investigations described in "How the Piano Came to Be Prepared."[78] However, those experiments—involving pie plates and nails—must have preceded the composition of *Imaginary Landscape No. 1*, the *First Construction (in Metal)*, and the *Second Construction* (1940), for all three of these works include a part for "string piano" (Cowell's term for a piano played otherwise than at the keyboard). Thus some strings are manually muted, while others are swept with a gong beater. The *First Construction* uses a metal rod, applied to the strings by an assistant, to produce a glissando of harmonics, and the *Second Construction* additionally employs two permanent mutes (a screw and a piece of cardboard).

By the time he came to write *Bacchanale*, Cage was already well versed in the techniques of piano alteration. The importance of the dance piece is threefold: first, the number and type of the preparations used is unprecedented in his music; second, it was his first solo piece for the instrument; and third, it was the first occasion on which he used the term "prepared piano." Nevertheless, the circumstances of its creation were somewhat serendipitous: Syvilla Fort had apparently asked for the score at very short notice. Cage divined the counts of the dance (rather than precomposing a square-root form) but was unable to write for his first choice of percussion ensemble due to the restrictions of the performance space. Failing also to devise an African tone row appropriate to the dance's subject, he "decided that what was wrong was the piano, not my efforts," and accordingly muted twelve pitches, mostly with weather stripping (a fibrous material designed to exclude drafts), though he also used one small bolt and one screw with loose nuts.[79] The physical placement of *Bacchanale*'s mutes is mainly left to the performer, though in most later prepared piano scores Cage is precise in his instructions. (Generally speaking, the mutes work best when positioned at or near the strings' nodal points, so as to emphasize particular harmonics.)

The consequences of piano preparation are several. First, it makes available to the composer an infinitely variable keyboard percussion instrument, whose thuds and plinks expand enormously the timbral resources of Western music and often suggest non-Western analogs. Second (and rather ironically), the piano—rather than percussion—became the medium through which Cage (in the words of the "Credo") came to effect the "contemporary transition from keyboard-influenced music to the all-sound music of the future." Third, and most importantly, compositions for the instrument (even more so than for percussion) began seriously to question the traditional relationship between notation, execution, and audition: music for the prepared piano is written as a conventional piano score, but because of the preparation, the sounds that emanate from the instrument bear little or no resemblance to those implied by the notation, except in rhythmic terms. Furthermore, owing to the differences of piano construction, even the most precise instructions for preparation cannot guarantee the production of absolute timbres. Thus the performer's role in the creation and selection of suitable instruments and preparations becomes paramount, and a distinct element of indeterminacy begins to subvert standard musical practices. As Cage later put it, "Notation became a way to produce something. The performer no longer had the impression that he would be able to hear the piece."[80]

Given the many positive aspects of Cage's sojourn in Seattle—apart from the musical developments described above, he had come into contact with the artists Morris Graves and Mark Tobey, and most particularly the dancer and choreographer Merce Cunningham (born 1919)—it is surprising that in the summer of 1940 he and Xenia moved to San Francisco. One reason may have been Cage's boredom with the routine accompanying of dance classes—which he described to Lou Harrison as "drudgery which I hate"—though the compensation afforded by the complementary concerts and other activities must surely have mitigated against this. Another reason may have been staff and administrative changes at the Cornish School that occurred during 1939. However, the most likely cause was Cage's ongoing wish to found a Center for Experimental Music: his summer concerts at Mills College in Oakland had been well received, and he no doubt saw Mills and its president, Aurelia Henry Reinhardt, as potentially supportive of the initiative.[81]

During the twelve months spent in San Francisco, Cage worked as a recreational leader for the Works Progress Administration, concertized with Harrison, and taught an extension course in percussion at Mills College.[82] But his institutional aspirations were frustrated, and another meeting with László Moholy-Nagy persuaded him to move to Chicago, where he taught a course in experimental music at the Bauhaus-influenced School of Design. While there, he again met up with Harry Partch (their first encounter was in New York eight years previously), worked as a dance accompanist at the University of Chicago, composed the second and third *Imaginary Landscapes*, and continued to give percussion concerts. Additionally, with the financial support of CBS Radio, he collaborated with Kenneth Patchen in a radio play, *The City Wears a Slouch Hat* (1942). The original 250–page score consisted of an extravagant and complex soundscape, a kind of early *musique concrète*. When the studio engineer pronounced it unfeasible, Cage wrote an hour's percussion music in four days. The resulting work achieved national broadcast and considerable public acclaim, especially in the West and Midwest. However, the Chicago School of Design, like Mills College, proved unable to fund Cage's dream of a Center for Experimental Music. And so, on the basis of the success of *The City Wears a Slouch Hat* and the promise of concerts and other opportunities, in the spring of 1942 the Cages moved—as it turned out, permanently—to the East Coast. As Cage later put it, he and Xenia decided that "we would come to New York and make our fortune."[83]

New York #1,
1942–54

Arrival

Despite the fact that they were almost penniless, John and Xenia Cage's decision to move to New York was not as whimsical or irrational as it may initially appear. At a practical level, New York was (as it still is) the most important and vibrant musical metropolis in the Americas. Furthermore, as a result of a chance meeting with Max Ernst and his wife Peggy Guggenheim, Cage had been offered accommodation and the prospect of a gallery concert in Manhattan. But perhaps even more compellingly, Cage may have been subconsciously—but inevitably—drawn to New York for other reasons. In his 1993 book *Creating Minds*, the social scientist Howard Gardner describes what he terms "the Exemplary Creator," a generalized and hypothetical portrait resulting from the common themes he identifies in the lives of such outstanding artists and thinkers as Sigmund Freud, Albert Einstein, Pablo Picasso, Igor Stravinsky, T. S. Eliot, Martha Graham, and Mahatma Gandhi. Gardner nicknames his creation "E. C." and makes her female, but the parallels between E. C. and J. C. are hard to miss.[1] Of particular note in the context of the present discussion is Gardner's assertion that, having outgrown her home environment, E. C. "ventures toward the city that is seen as a center of vital activities for her domain." For Cage, this was New York; thus, following his earlier sojourn in 1934, it was natural that he should return there so that he might find—in Gardner's words—"a set of peers who [shared] the same interests" and with whom he might "[organize] institutions, [issue] manifestos, and [stimulate] one another to new heights."[2] However, this meeting with a peer group did not truly occur until 1950.

The Cages' actual arrival in New York was somewhat bizarre. As Cage describes it in *Silence*, he and Xenia had only twenty-five cents between them. Having been promised a room by Ernst, they used a nickel to phone him. Ernst didn't recognize Cage's voice but invited him over for cocktails the following evening. "I went back to Xenia and told her what had happened. She said, 'Call him back. We have everything to gain and nothing to lose.' I did. He said, 'Oh! It's you. We've been waiting for you for weeks. Your room's ready. Come right over.'" Initially, all went well: through Peggy Guggenheim, the Cages met a panoply of contemporary artists and other figures, including André Breton, Joseph Cornell, Marcel Duchamp, Piet Mondrian, Jackson Pollock, Virgil Thomson, and even Gypsy Rose Lee.[3] Guggenheim arranged for Cage's percussion instruments to be transported from Chicago and intended that a percussion concert should open her new Art of This Century Gallery.

After this auspicious start, however, things began quickly to go wrong, possibly as a result of Cage's naivete and inexperience in dealing with "the great and the good." In an unusual display of thoughtlessness, he set up a percussion concert at the rival Museum of Modern Art (MoMA) as part of the League of Composers' twentieth-anniversary program. Guggenheim was livid: she cancelled the Art of This Century date and made it clear that the Cages' residency in her apartment was temporary. On top of this, a meeting with Varèse went badly (he and his wife had been affronted by Cage and Harrison using the Varèsian term "organized sound" in connection with their recent recording of Harrison's *Simfony #13*, though this rift was later healed); a putative engagement as an accompanist for Martha Graham's dance classes fell through; and the acclaim that had greeted *The City Wears a Slouch Hat* in the Midwest was countered by East Coast indifference. A few months after their arrival in New York, not only had the Cages failed to make their fortune; they had also become bereft of accommodation and income. Despite his initial reaction—bursting into tears in front of Marcel Duchamp—Cage's belief that he had a guardian angel helped him through this temporary crisis.[4] Accommodation was provided by the dancer Jean Erdman and her husband, the mythologist Joseph Campbell. Through Erdman, Cage renewed his acquaintance with Merce Cunningham, which resulted in commissions for dance scores. Following a series of begging letters to friends in Chicago and elsewhere, around fifty dollars was gratefully received, and Cage was able, once again, to undertake research for his father, who was engaged in military work. This last activity spared Cage being drafted, America having entered World War II at the end of 1941.

The music that Cage wrote during 1941–42 reflects his circumstances: of the seven works that immediately follow *The City Wears a Slouch Hat*, all but one are dance scores, for which he was paid at a rate of five dollars per minute of music, and four—*Totem Ancestor, And the Earth Shall Bear Again, Primitive,* and *In the Name of the Holocaust* (all 1942)—are for prepared piano.[5] The dance pieces are mainly structured according to the dancers' counts, and those for prepared piano are generally sparse both texturally and timbrally. Like the slightly earlier *Imaginary Landscape No. 3, In the Name of the Holocaust* is a personal reaction to the horrors of war. Similar in tone is *Credo in Us* (also known, punningly, as *Credo in U.S.;* 1942): written for four percussionists and unfolding in accordance with a bizarre, almost Joycean, scenario by Cunningham, the work is unusual in the degree to which Cage uses existing music and existing styles to parodistic (or even possibly political) purposes.[6] The stylistic references in this "suite of satirical character" are to Stravinsky, folk song, cowboy music, jazz, blues, and ragtime. Player 4 has the choice of using either a radio or a record player, and if the latter is employed, Cage suggests that the LPs played are "some classic: e.g. Dvořák, Beethoven, Sibelius, or Shostakovich." *Forever and Sunsmell* (1942), written to accompany a dance by Erdman, for two percussionists and voice, is in two parts that are connected by an unaccompanied hummed interlude; the text is by e. e. cummings, from "26" in *50 Poems* (1941). Another asyntactic source, James Joyce's *Finnegans Wake,* provided the words for the folk-like melody of the song *The Wonderful Widow of Eighteen Springs* (commissioned by Janet Fairbanks; 1942), whose accompaniment—perhaps following Fischinger's suggestion—is tapped out on the lid and body of a closed piano. *Finnegans Wake* assumed major importance for Cage in his later career.

A particular focus of Cage's activities was the Museum of Modern Art concert, which took place on February 7, 1943, under the auspices of the League of Composers. Despite "the difficulties involved in twelve people getting together in New York City for something as uncommercial as a non-union rehearsal," extensive preparations were made.[7] The group of thirteen performers (including Xenia Cage and Merce Cunningham) put together a program featuring works by Jose Ardévol (*Preludio a 11*), Henry Cowell (premiere of *Ostinato Pianissimo*), Lou Harrison (*Counterdance in the Spring* and *Canticle*), Amadeo Roldán (*Ritmicas V and VI*), and Cage himself (*First Construction (in Metal), Imaginary Landscape*

No. 3, and the first performance of *Amores* [1943]). The full resources of Cage's battery—from anvils to woodblocks, flowerpots to brake drums, and rice bowls to thundersheets—were utilized, and the CBS sound-effects department helped out with the electrical equipment for the *Imaginary Landscape*. The concert was an artistic and critical success and was featured the following month in a two-page spread in *Life* magazine, which described Cage as "a patient, humorous, 30–year-old Californian . . . the most active percussion musician in the U.S." Beneath the tuxedos and concert frocks, however, passions were rising.

Crisis

Cage's new work for the MoMA concert, *Amores*, was—like some of his percussion instruments—partly recycled: the first and last movements are solos for prepared piano, and in between are two trios for percussion, the second of which is the "Waltz" from the 1936 *Trio*. The title of the work—possibly alluding to a sequence of eight poems in cummings's 1923 collection *Tulips and Chimneys*—was meant, according to Cage, to be concerned with "the quietness between lovers."[8] But the appearance of the two trios also possibly alludes to the fact that John, Xenia, and Merce were in love with each other: reacquaintance had led to the (re)kindling of affection. Initially, the dynamics of the *ménage à trois* were equable; but subsequently, Cage realized that he was more drawn to Cunningham than to his wife.[9] John and Xenia separated in 1945 and divorced soon after. A sense of the tensions that developed during these two years may be gleaned from some of the titles and topics of Cage's works, though this inevitably involves speculation, given Cage's lifelong reluctance to discuss this aspect of his private life.

At the most obvious level, Cage stated in the 1948 lecture "A Composer's Confessions" that *The Perilous Night* (1943–44), a six-movement concert work for prepared piano, "concerned the loneliness and terror that comes to one when love becomes unhappy."[10] One might argue that this "lost, sad, and rather desperate piece" is simply a response to the Irish folk text that inspired it;[11] but Cage could have chosen any other text as a source of inspiration. Similarly, the title of a five-minute prepared-piano work written for Xenia to play—*A Valentine out of Season* (1944)—is pregnant with meaning. In retrospect, numerous other works of this period, intended for the concert platform and the dance stage, seem also to hint darkly at the unraveling of one relationship and the knitting of another: *Our Spring Will Come* (dance; prepared piano; 1943), *She Is Asleep* (concert; voice, percussion, and piano, prepared or not; 1943), *A Room* (concert; piano, prepared or not; 1943), *Tossed as It is Untroubled (Meditation)* (dance; prepared piano; 1943),

Four Walls (dance; voice and piano; text by Cunningham; 1944), *Soliloquy* (concert; piano; 1945), *Mysterious Adventure* (dance; prepared piano; 1945).

Speculation aside, the crisis in Cage's private life seems to have spurred rather than hindered his creativity. Between the MoMA concert in February 1943 and the premiere of the orchestral ballet *The Seasons* in May 1947, Cage composed almost thirty pieces. Most are admittedly short (under five minutes in length) and for limited resources (over twenty are for solo keyboard), but this is still an impressive body of music. Four technical features are worthy of comment. First, by comparison with his earlier percussion music, the vast majority of the rhythmic writing here is relatively simple, often featuring repetitive figures or ostinatos. This may be a pragmatic result of it being composed for solo performer rather than ensemble, but the effect is still surprising: the polyrhythmic density of the *First* and *Third Constructions*, for example, is replaced by simple duple relationships between the hands. Alternatively, Cage may have been constricted by his limitations as a pianist: he was clearly very competent, but, as noted earlier, he was "more interested in sight-reading than in running up and down the scales. Being a virtuoso didn't interest [him] at all."[12] Another explanation may lie in the timbral complexity of music emanating from the prepared piano and the consequent need to reduce the amount of aural information being fed to the listener, though one could easily argue that the music for percussion ensemble is also timbrally complex. Perhaps the simplest rationale for Cage's newfound rhythmic simplicity is the function of most of these works as accompaniments to dances. Performers usually require rhythmically simple music to best coordinate their movements with the score, and in his "Notes on Compositions I" Cage identifies a number of pieces from this period—including *Totem Ancestor, Root of an Unfocus, Daughters of the Lonesome Isle, Experience 1* and *2, Mysterious Adventure,* and *Ophelia*—that either "followed the rhythmic structure given by Merce Cunningham" (in the case of *Mysterious Adventure*) or had "a phraseology corresponding to that of the dance by Jean Erdman" (in the case of *Ophelia*), to cite only two of Cage's annotations.[13] Contradicting even this argument, though, is the equally simple rhythmic profile of such concert pieces as *Prelude for Meditation* (1944), *A Valentine out of Season* (1944), *A Book of Music* (1944), and the *Three Dances* (1945)—both of these latter works for two prepared pianos and written for the professional duo of Arthur Gold and Robert Fizdale—and especially *A Room* (1943).

Linked to the rhythmic simplicity of these works—and even more surprising, given the predominant dissonance of Cage's music of the previous decade—is their consonant simplicity. The compositions for unprepared piano (such as *Triple-Paced No. 1* [1943] and *Soliloquy*) are implicitly tonal, and in some cases—harking back to the parodistic style of *Credo in Us*—are overt in their references to jazz, a genre Cage supposedly disliked. Furthermore, although their timbres are of necessity nontonal, many of the prepared piano pieces—especially *Our Spring Will Come* and *Prelude for Meditation*—are notated quasi-tonally or pentatonically, while the third of the *Three Dances* even opens with a quotation from Virgil Thomson's *Hymn Tune Symphony*.[14] It would seem that Cage was—as he had promised Schoenberg—beating his head against the wall of harmony and, at the very least, distressing its surface.[15]

The third technical feature of these works worthy of comment is the increasingly detailed nature of their piano preparations. As noted previously in the discussion of *Bacchanale*, Cage's earliest preparations are simple, with the physical placement of the mutes left mainly to the performer. Though some later preparations—such as those of *Root of an Unfocus* (1944), *Prelude for Meditation*, and particularly *The Unavailable Memory Of* (1944)—remain uncomplicated, Cage almost always gives precise instructions as to their positioning (for example, weather stripping, strings 1–2, 3 ¾" from damper). In some other pieces, however, the number and type of preparations is considerable: for *Mysterious Adventure*, Cage alters twenty-seven pitches, and several of these are subjected to triple preparation (three separate preparations are applied to the strings of a single pitch). For *Daughters of the Lonesome Isle* (1945), there are thirty-nine prepared pitches, many of which are double preparations. The muting materials used in these two works range from the familiar bolts, screws, nuts, and rubber through to the fiddly "rubber-wrapped wood with bolt" (*Mysterious Adventure*, A♭ below middle C, strings 2–3, 5 ⅜" from damper). Elsewhere, we find two thicknesses of woolen material, a piece of plastic (both in *And the Earth Shall Bear Again*), wood and cloth (*The Perilous Night*), pennies, slit bamboo (both in *A Valentine out of Season*), and weather stripping (several works). The timbral palette resulting from the use of these materials is gloriously rich and infinitely subtle (not least in the possibilities created for the contrasting of timbral groups and in the occasional juxtaposition of prepared and unprepared sounds). Conversely, however, in several works—such as *The Unavailable Memory Of* and *Root of an Unfocus*—Cage deliberately employs only limited gamuts of pitches/timbres, a compositional restriction that links his work to that of Harrison and which becomes ever more important in Cage's music later in the decade.[16] One further detail: *In the Name of the Holocaust* and *Triple-Paced No. 1* find Cage borrowing various of Cowell's piano-manipulation techniques, such as plucked notes, forearm clusters, and swept strings.

The final technical point relates to Cage's continuing use of square-root form. Inevitably, as Cage sometimes points out in his program notes for those works, many of the dance pieces are structured concretely, via the dancers' counts, rather than abstractly.[17] But in his concert music as well as some of the dances, micro-macrocosmic forms maintain. Thus the final movement of the concert piece *Amores* has a rhythmic structure of 3 : 3 : 2 : 2, and the dance work *Tossed as It Is Untroubled* is arranged as 7 : 7. One refinement of square-root form that starts to emerge at this period is in its relationship to real time. Formerly, Cage had retained the given durational structure regardless of changes of tempo: thus in the *First Construction (in Metal)*, the basic phraseology of 4 : 3 : 2 : 3 : 4 remains intact throughout the work, though the tempo varies considerably to either side of the initial quarter-note = 96. Consequently, the integrity of the given durational relationships is compromised as the basic pulse alters. In the first and second of the *Three Dances*, however, it is the phrase structure that is altered in accordance with the changes of tempo, so that the durational relationships remain constant: the first movement (at 88 beats per minute) is 30 x 30 measures in length, and has a phrase structure of 2 : 5 : 2 : 2 : 6 : 2 : 2 : 7 : 2. When, for the second movement, the tempo increases to 114 beats per minute, Cage accordingly changes the length to 39 x 39 and the phrase structure to 3 : 6 : 3 : 3 : 7 : 3 : 3 : 8 : 3.[18] In some later works, this procedure on occasion leads to highly complex fractional proportions.

Eastern Influences

Following his separation from Xenia, Cage moved to the first of several apartments he occupied on the Lower East Side of Manhattan; one was described in glowing terms in a June 1946 article in *Junior Harper's Bazaar.*[19] Their locations—mostly facing the East River rather than Manhattan, and looking toward and beyond Europe rather than into and across America—are perhaps significant in light of the aesthetic changes that were about to engulf him. Unsurprisingly, given his sexual reorientation and the breakup of his ten-year marriage, Cage entered a period of intense and emotional self-examination. The most obvious external manifestations of this crisis are the works he composed, which not only feature emotive titles and topics but also attempt to express emotions, ideas, and beliefs. As Calvin Tomkins puts it, "Much of the music [Cage] had written in Chicago and New York had been an attempt to express his own personal ideas. *Imaginary Landscape No. 3*, with its thunderous sound effects and loud electronic buzzes, was intended to suggest war and devastation. In *Amores* . . . Cage had tried to express his belief that even in wartime beauty remains in intimate interactions between individuals."[20] It was supremely ironic, then, that at the very time when Cage was at his most emotionally intense, he came to realize that his music was not achieving its purpose. According to Tomkins, one critic described the last movement of *The Perilous Night* as sounding like "a woodpecker in a church belfry." Cage's misery was thus compounded: "I had poured a great deal of emotion into the piece, and obviously I wasn't communicating this at all. Or else, I thought, if I *were* communicating, then all artists must be speaking a different language, and thus speaking only for themselves. The whole musical situation struck me more and more as a Tower of Babel."[21] Alternatively, as Cage puts it in "An Autobiographical Statement," "I could not accept the academic idea that the purpose of music was communication, because I noticed that when I conscientiously wrote something sad, people and critics were often apt to laugh. I determined to give up composition unless I could find a better reason for doing it than communication."[22]

One possible solution to Cage's problems lay in psychoanalysis, and on the advice of several friends he consulted a Jungian analyst.[23] However, such a course of action was doomed from the start: Cage "had a chip on [his] shoulder about psychoanalysis" and was aware of Rilke's view: "I'm sure they would remove my devils, but I fear they would offend my angels." Thus, "When I went to the analyst for some kind of preliminary meeting, he said 'I'll be able to fix you so that you'll write much more music than you do now.' I said, 'Good heavens! I already write too much, it seems to me.' That promise of his put me off."[24] As might be surmised from this story, Cage was not without support at this time. Although "the quietness of [my] retreat . . . on the East River in Lower Manhattan" encouraged introspection, "Lou Harrison . . . [and] Merton Brown, another composer and close friend, were always ready to talk and ask and discuss any question relative to music with me."[25] Besides these two—Harrison had moved to New York in the summer of 1943—there was, of course, Cunningham, as well as Virgil Thomson and Henry Cowell, the latter having been resident in New York State since his release from San Quentin in 1940. In 1945, Cage, Cowell, Harrison, and Thomson co-composed a series of *Party Pieces (Sonorous and Exquisite Corpses)*, on the surrealist model, which must have provided Cage with some amusement and solace.

However, once again it was Cage's guardian angel who ultimately came to his aid in the form of a young Indian woman, Geeta Sarabhai. (In his 1948 lecture "A Composer's Confessions," Cage writes that Sarabhai "came like an angel from India.")[26] Cage was already familiar with some aspects of Asian philosophy and aesthetics: in 1943, Harrison had shown him the ancient Chinese book of oracles, the *I Ching*, and while at the Cornish School Cage had attended a lecture by Nancy Wilson Ross on "Zen Buddhism and Dada."[27] Subsequently, Cage's brief 1942 residency at the apartment of Jean Erdman and Joseph Campbell led to an exchange of ideas with Campbell, who introduced Cage to Ananda K. Coomaraswamy's *The Transformation of Nature in Art*, a source to which Cage referred in his 1946 article "The East in the West."[28] One of Cage's mantras in later life was a phrase drawn from Coomaraswamy's book—"Art is the imitation of Nature in her manner of operation"—and many of his subsequent aesthetic tenets are derived from Coomaraswamy's writings.[29]

Consequently, in Cage's words, "oriental philosophy took the place for me of psychoanalysis," and his somewhat fortuitous meeting with Geeta Sarabhai was an important part of that process.[30] Following eight years of traditional Hindustani musical training in singing, drumming, and theory, Sarabhai had come to America to better understand a culture that she believed was threatening that of her own country. Shortly after her arrival in New York in mid-1946, she was introduced to Cage by the artist Isamu Noguchi: "'John very readily offered to teach me what he had learnt from Schoenberg . . . [in return, he said] that if I taught him Indian music there would be no question of payment.'"[31] In fact, it was Indian philosophy and aesthetics rather than music that Sarabhai taught Cage. Over a five-month period, and often with Harrison in attendance, she and Cage met several times each week. Given Cage's contemporaneous concerns regarding the communication of expression in music, it was inevitable that at some point he should ask Sarabhai about the function of music in India. Her reply, based on her teacher's views, was that the purpose of music is to concentrate the mind; this chimed in with a passage Harrison had discovered in the writings of the seventeenth-century English musician Thomas Mace, which Cage in "A Composer's Confessions" summarizes thus: "[T]he purpose of music [is] to season and sober the mind, thus making it susceptible of divine influences, and elevating one's affections to goodness."[32]

Before returning to India at the end of 1946, Sarabhai presented Cage with a copy of *The Gospel of Sri Ramakrishna*, the predominantly spiritual nature of which also helped Cage in his process of inner healing: "When I was growing up, church and Sunday School became devoid of anything [I] needed. . . . I was almost forty years old before I discovered what I needed—in Oriental thought. . . . I was starved—I was thirsty. These things had all been in the Protestant Church, but they had been there in a form in which I couldn't use them."[33] Or, as David Patterson puts it, "*The Gospel of Sri Ramakrishna* was essential to [Cage], providing inspiration as well as general relief from the tensions surrounding his more personal transitions of the mid-1940s."[34]

There is a footnote to Cage's period of crisis that should be mentioned here as an example of his generosity to others. In 1947, Lou Harrison suffered a nervous breakdown, mainly as a result of the stress of living in New York. In the words of Leta Miller and Fredric Lieberman, "Cage immediately came to Lou's aid [and] unbeknownst to Harrison . . . sought help from Lou's friends, including Ives." Harrison's hospital bills were thus covered; he made a full recovery and in 1951 was able to exchange urban frenzy for rural tranquility, initially through a position Cage found for him at Black Mountain College."[35] Harrison never forgot these acts of kindness, and although an aesthetic gap opened between him and Cage from the 1950s onwards, he always spoke and wrote of Cage with huge affection and respect.

Newly fired by his meeting with Sarabhai, Cage embarked on what he described as "eighteen months of studying oriental and medieval Christian philosophical mysticism."[36] Among the sources he consulted were the sermons of the fourteenth-century German mystic Meister Eckhart, Aldous Huxley's *The Perennial Philosophy*, Coomaraswamy's *The Dance of Shiva*, and, subsequently, a variety of Taoist, Buddhist, and especially Zen texts. He also began, despite his earlier unhelpful experience of psychoanalysis, to read Carl Jung's writings on the integration of personality. Cage seems to have accepted Jung's view that the "two principal parts of each personality [are] the conscious mind and the unconscious, and [that] these are split and dispersed in most of us, in countless ways and directions." Applying this to his own situation and beliefs, Cage declared, "The function of music, like that of any other healthy occupation, is to help to bring those separate parts back together again. Music does this by providing a moment when, awareness of time and space being lost, the multiplicity of elements which make up an individual become integrated and he is one." Cage adds a cautionary note—"This only happens if, in the presence of music, one does not allow himself to fall into laziness or distraction"—before coming to the conclusion that "[i]f one makes music, as the Orient would say, *disinterestedly*, that is, without concern for money or fame but simply for the love of making it, it is an integrating activity and one will find moments in his life that are complete and fulfilled."[37]

The musical and other results of Cage's aesthetic and philosophical discoveries were various and varied, and to a considerable extent they are endemic (though not always fully acknowledged) in all of his subsequent work. In compositional terms, a kind of stylistic bifurcation appears to occur. On the one hand, Cage continued to write pieces whose sound world—not least timbrally—developed that of such recent prepared-piano works as *A Book of Music* and *Daughters of the Lonesome Isle*. This series of pieces includes *Music for Marcel Duchamp* (1947) for prepared piano, *Dream* (1948) for piano, *In a Landscape* (1948) for piano or harp, and the *Suite* (1948) for toy piano or piano. *Music for Marcel Duchamp* was written to accompany a sequence devised by Duchamp for Hans Richter's surrealist film *Dreams That Money Can Buy*. *Dream, In a Landscape*, and the *Suite* are all dance scores, written for Louise Lippold (*In a Landscape*) and Merce Cunningham. Their shared flowing lyricism might therefore be attributed to their essentially programmatic genesis, though they all to a greater or lesser extent also make use of the kinds of scalic patterns that were the basis of the abstract, deliberately Mozartian *A Book of Music*. But while *Dream* and *In a Landscape* are structured according to the dancers' counts, *Music for Marcel Duchamp* and the *Suite*—also like *A Book of Music*—use micro-macrocosmic forms, that for the *Suite* being 7 : 7 : 6 : 6 : 4. Additionally related to this "lyrical" sequence of pieces are another Cunningham dance score, *Experiences No. 2* (1948) for solo voice (which again sets a text by e. e. cummings), and the *Nocturne* for violin and piano (1947).

In contrast to the flowing qualities of these works is the much more static nature of two linked compositions, the *Two Pieces for Piano* (1946) and the orchestral ballet *The Seasons* (1947). The *Two Pieces* were completed in August 1946 and therefore probably predate Cage's meeting with Geeta Sarabhai. Although each includes a quasi-melodic skeleton, it is the brittle, chordal, dynamically unpredictable, and mostly dissonant surface that catches the ear's attention, diverting it from the simple lyricism that exists subcutaneously. Written in square-root form (3 : 5 : 2 for I; 2 ¼ : 3 ¾: 1 ¾ : 2 ¼ for II), the sense of stasis is heightened by Cage's use of extended silences (some lasting five measures) in the first piece and of extended chords (some of which progressively thin out) in the second. These curious and fascinating works, which look forward to Cage's *Concerto for Prepared Piano and Orchestra* (1950–51) and the music of Morton Feldman, served as studies for sections of *The Seasons*.

The sixteen-minute score of *The Seasons* was commissioned through Lincoln Kirstein by the Ballet Society in New York; it was choreographed by Cunningham, and the scenery and costumes were by Isamu Noguchi. Unlike the *Two Pieces*, *The Seasons* is overt in its debt to Cage's recent immersion in Indian philosophy and aesthetics. Its implicitly cyclic structure is arranged in nine sections: four bear the titles of the seasons, and—in accordance with the traditional Indian view—each season is associated with a dynamic quality: thus winter (section 2) is quiescence, spring (section 4) is creation, summer (section 6) is preservation, and fall (section 8) is destruction. Before each of the seasonal movements comes a shorter prelude, while the final movement is a repeat of the opening Prelude I, emphasizing the work's cyclicism. Cage organizes his material in two ways. First, the large- and small-scale shape of the work is controlled by micro-macrocosmic form (though at the microcosmic level the proportions are adjusted to reflect changes in tempo). This generates the following overall structure:

TABLE 1. *Overall structure of Cage,* The Seasons.

Movement	Macrocosmic Proportion
Prelude I	2
Winter	2
Prelude II	1
Spring	3
Prelude III	2
Summer	4
Prelude IV	1
Fall	3
Finale (Prelude I)	1

Second, in a manner similar to that employed in *The Unavailable Memory Of* and *Root of an Unfocus,* the musical material is taken from a fixed gamut of single pitches, intervals, and more complex chords, though the timbral qualities of the gamut are varied through changes of orchestration.[38] Cage saw the composition of his first orchestral work as a considerable challenge and stated that it was, from his point of view, "highly experimental . . . the sound of a flute, of the violins, of a harp, of a trombone, suggest to me most attractive adventures."[39] The first performance of the ballet was well received, with critics drawing attention to its instrumental colors and comparing Cage's writing to that of Ravel, Schoenberg, and Stravinsky.[40]

Dominating this period, however, and to a considerable extent linking together the two strands of Cage's output discussed above, is one of his most famous (and extensive) works, the *Sonatas and Interludes* for prepared piano (1946–48). Commenced in February 1946, the composition of the twenty movements of this hour-long piece occupied Cage for just over two years. The piano preparation was his most complex to date, involving the alteration of forty-five pitches; about a third of these involve double or triple preparations, and the materials employed range from screws and bolts, sometimes with appended nuts, to rubber, plastic, and an eraser (the table of preparations is reproduced on page 41). Drawing again on the writings of Coomaraswamy—in this case his monograph *The Dance of Shiva*—Cage sought in the *Sonatas and Interludes* "to express in music the 'permanent emotions' of Indian tradition: the heroic, the erotic, the wondrous, the mirthful, sorrow, fear, anger, the odious and their common tendency toward tranquility."[41] According to David Revill, the central emotion, tranquility, became Cage's lodestar and "the way to make himself susceptible [to the] 'divine influences'" cited by Thomas Mace.[42]

The *Sonatas and Interludes* are arranged in a particularly intricate formal structure: there are sixteen sonatas and four interludes, and they are laid out palindromically, with groups of four sonatas either followed or preceded by a single interlude. Despite this formality, there is no apparent or definitive association between particular emotions and individual movements, though each of the twenty numbers possesses a distinctive emotional character, conveyed through tempo, rhythm, timbre, and dynamics. There is no overall musical structure (i.e., a meta-micro-macrocosmic arrangement), though each of the individual movements has its own square-root form. However, these proportions are complicated somewhat by Cage's additional use of binary and ternary forms and by his employment, in some instances, of fractional numbers in the unit size and in the macrocosmic proportions by which those units are multiplied. These various structural elements are summarized in table 2.

One final complicating detail results from the fact that Sonatas XIV and XV were conceived as a pair and named "Gemini" after a sculpture by Cage's friend Richard Lippold. They share certain structural features as well as—in their second halves—musical material.

In their musical language the *Sonatas and Interludes* cover a huge range, which summarizes and extends considerably Cage's prepared-piano writing of the previous eight years. Repetition and ostinatos are often in evidence, but there are also delicate quasi-monodic textures reminiscent of *Tossed as It Is Untroubled* and *Music for Marcel Duchamp* and many moments of actual or implied silence, evoking the stasis of the contemporaneous *Two Pieces for Piano*. Furthermore, as David Bernstein has noted, there are once again distinctly tonal aspects to the writing, in its notation and in the timbral groupings that result.[43] Overall, the work achieves a fine and fascinating balance between familiar and unfamiliar, East and West, and tradition and experiment, which Virgil Thomson eulogized as "'[d]elightful, varied, sprightly, recalling in both sound and shape the esercizi . . . for harpsichord of Domenico Scarlatti.'"[44]

By the time of Maro Ajemian's premiere of the *Sonatas and Interludes* in January 1949, Cage had not only successfully weathered his personal and musical crisis but had emerged from it refreshed and reinvigorated. His continuing immersion in Asian philosophy and aesthetics had provided a new focus for his work, and

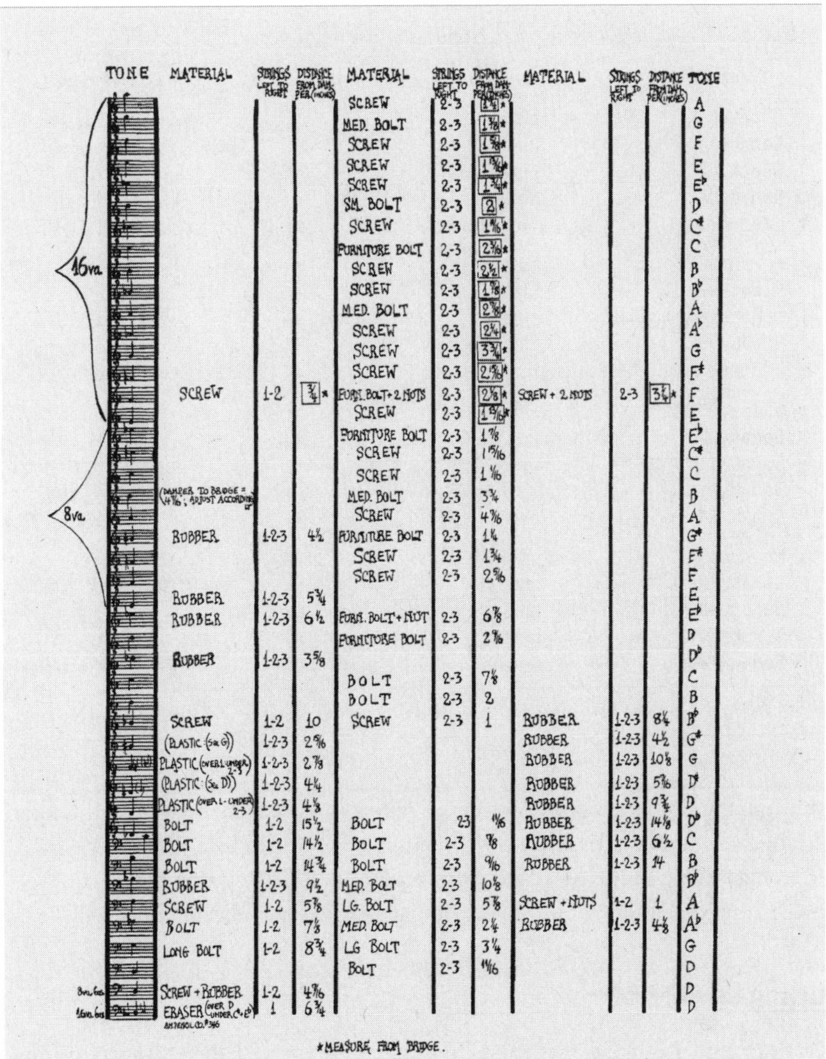

TONE	MATERIAL	STRINGS LEFT TO RIGHT	DISTANCE FROM DAMPER (INCHES)	MATERIAL	STRINGS LEFT TO RIGHT	DISTANCE FROM DAMPER (INCHES)	MATERIAL	STRINGS LEFT TO RIGHT	DISTANCE FROM DAMPER (INCHES)	TONE
				SCREW	2-3	1 3/4*				A
				MED. BOLT	2-3	1 3/8*				G
				SCREW	2-3	1 7/8*				F
				SCREW	2-3	1 9/16*				E
				SCREW	2-3	1 3/4*				E♭
				SM. BOLT	2-3	2*				D
				SCREW	2-3	1 9/16*				C♯
				FURNITURE BOLT	2-3	2 3/16*				C
				SCREW	2-3	2 1/2*				B
				SCREW	2-3	1 7/8*				B♭
				MED. BOLT	2-3	2 3/8*				A
				SCREW	2-3	2 1/4*				A♭
				SCREW	2-3	3 3/4*				G
				SCREW	2-3	2 5/16*				F♯
	SCREW	1-2	3/4*	FURN. BOLT + 2 NUTS	2-3	2 1/8*	SCREW + 2 NUTS	2-3	3 3/4*	F
				SCREW	2-3	1 15/16*				E
				FURNITURE BOLT	2-3	1 7/8				E♭
				SCREW	2-3	1 15/16				C♯
				SCREW	2-3	1 1/16				C
	(DAMPER TO BRIDGE = 4 5/16; ADJUST ACCORDINGLY)			MED. BOLT	2-3	3 3/4				B
				SCREW	2-3	4 5/16				A
	RUBBER	1-2-3	4 1/2	FURNITURE BOLT	2-3	1 1/4				G♯
				SCREW	2-3	1 3/4				F♯
				SCREW	2-3	2 5/16				F
	RUBBER	1-2-3	5 3/4							E
	RUBBER	1-2-3	6 1/2	FURN. BOLT + NUT	2-3	6 7/8				E♭
				FURNITURE BOLT	2-3	2 9/16				D
	RUBBER	1-2-3	3 5/8							D♭
				BOLT	2-3	7 1/8				C
				BOLT	2-3	2				B
	SCREW	1-2	10	SCREW	2-3	1	RUBBER	1-2-3	8 1/4	B♭
	(PLASTIC (SEE G))	1-2-3	2 5/16				RUBBER	1-2-3	4 1/2	G♯
	PLASTIC (OVER 1 - UNDER 2-3)	1-2-3	2 7/8				RUBBER	1-2-3	10 1/8	G
	(PLASTIC (SEE D))	1-2-3	4 1/4				RUBBER	1-2-3	5 5/16	D♯
	PLASTIC (OVER 1 - UNDER 2-3)	1-2-3	4 1/8				RUBBER	1-2-3	9 3/4	D
	BOLT	1-2	15 1/2	BOLT	2-3	11/16	RUBBER	1-2-3	14 1/8	D♭
	BOLT	1-2	14 1/2	BOLT	2-3	7/8	RUBBER	1-2-3	6 1/2	C
	BOLT	1-2	14 3/4	BOLT	2-3	9/16	RUBBER	1-2-3	14	B
	RUBBER	1-2-3	9 1/2	MED. BOLT	2-3	10 1/8				B♭
	SCREW	1-2	5 7/8	LG. BOLT	2-3	5 7/8	SCREW + NUTS	1-2	1	A
	BOLT	1-2	7 1/8	MED. BOLT	2-3	2 1/4	RUBBER	1-2-3	4 5/8	A♭
	LONG BOLT	1-2	8 3/4	LG BOLT	2-3	3 1/4				G
				BOLT	2-3	11/16				D
8va bassa	SCREW + RUBBER	1-2	4 7/16							D
16va bassa	ERASER (OVER D, UNDER C♯ + E♭) AM. PENCIL CO. #346	1	6 3/4							D

*MEASURE FROM BRIDGE.

John Cage, table of preparations from Sonatas and Interludes. *Edition Peters No. 6755. ©1960 Henmar Press Inc., New York. Used by permission of Peters Edition Limited, London.*

TABLE 2: *Overall structure of Cage,* Sonatas and Interludes.

MOVEMENT	FORM	UNIT SIZE	PROPORTIONS
Sonata I	binary	7	$1\frac{1}{4}$:$\frac{3}{4}$:$1\frac{1}{4}$:$\frac{3}{4}$:$1\frac{1}{2}$:$1\frac{1}{2}$
Sonata II	binary	$7\frac{3}{4}$	$1\frac{1}{2}$:$1\frac{1}{2}$:$2\frac{3}{8}$:$2\frac{3}{8}$
Sonata III	binary	$8\frac{1}{2}$	1:1:$3\frac{1}{4}$:$3\frac{1}{4}$
Sonata IV	binary	10	3:3:2:2
Interlude 1	through-composed	10	$1\frac{1}{2}$:$1\frac{1}{2}$:2:$1\frac{1}{2}$:$1\frac{1}{2}$:2
Sonata V	binary	9	2:2:$2\frac{1}{2}$:$2\frac{1}{2}$
Sonata VI	binary	6	$2\frac{2}{3}$:$2\frac{2}{3}$:$\frac{1}{3}$:$\frac{1}{3}$
Sonata VII	binary	6	2:2:1:1
Sonata VIII	binary	7	2:2:$1\frac{1}{2}$:$1\frac{1}{2}$
Interlude 2	through-composed	8	unclear
Interlude 3	4-part: AABBCCDD	7	$1\frac{1}{4}$:$1\frac{1}{4}$:1:1:$\frac{3}{4}$:$\frac{3}{4}$:$\frac{1}{2}$:$\frac{1}{2}$
Sonata IX	ternary: ABBCC	8	1:2:2:$1\frac{1}{2}$:$1\frac{1}{2}$
Sonata X	ternary: AABBC	6	1:1:1:1:2
Sonata XI	ternary: AABCC	10	2:2:3:$1\frac{1}{2}$:$1\frac{1}{2}$
Sonata XII	binary	9	2:2:$2\frac{1}{2}$:$2\frac{1}{2}$
Interlude 4	4-part: AABBCCDD	$8\frac{1}{2}$	1:1:1:1:1:1:$1\frac{1}{4}$:$1\frac{1}{4}$
Sonata XIII	binary	10	$1\frac{1}{2}$:$1\frac{1}{2}$:$3\frac{1}{2}$:$3\frac{1}{2}$
Sonata XIV	binary	10	2:2:3:3
Sonata XV	binary	10	2:2:3:3
Sonata XVI	binary	10	$3\frac{1}{2}$:$3\frac{1}{2}$:$1\frac{1}{2}$:$1\frac{1}{2}$

Note: Based on James Pritchett, *The Music of John Cage,* 30, 32-33.

through the support of such prominent critics as Thomson, he was beginning to establish a notable presence on the contemporary American musical scene. As Ross Parmenter of the *New York Times* put it, "'Mr. Cage is one of this country's finest composers and . . . his invention has now been vindicated musically.'"[45]

Giving Up Control

By the summer of 1948, Cage and Cunningham were well on the way to forming what was eventually called the Merce Cunningham Dance Company. They had been giving joint recitals since the spring of 1944, and much of Cage's music of the later 1940s was triggered by the needs of Cunningham's choreography. Their collaborations were already premised in the notion that music and dance should be created independently and only brought together at a late stage in rehearsals, this being made possible through micro-macrocosmic structuring.[46] Cage and Cunningham also collaborated in seeking out new opportunities for the dissemination of their work: one result of this was a joint visit in August 1948 to Black Mountain College, a small and idealistic institution in North Carolina.[47] During this visit, the duo gave a performance, and Cage took part in a panel discussion, as well as completing *Experiences No. 2*, *In a Landscape*, and the *Suite*. He also talked the college into mounting a short festival devoted to the work of Erik Satie, as part of which Cage gave several lectures; it was originally intended that these should subsequently be published by Black Mountain.

Cage had probably first discovered Satie's music in the 1930s and had subsequently been encouraged in his interests by Thomson. The Black Mountain festival included a performance of the theater piece *Le piège de Méduse* (1913/21), in an English translation by Mary Caroline Richards: Cage played the piano, and among the performers were Cunningham, Elaine de Kooning, and Buckminster Fuller; the set and costumes were by Willem and Elaine de Kooning. Another element in the festival was a series of lectures delivered by Cage, the longest of which—"Defense of Satie"—is included in Richard Kostelanetz's *John Cage*.[48] In this lecture, Cage praises Satie and Anton Webern (1883–1945) for what he identifies as their common interest (shared with the Orient) in defining "the parts of a composition . . . by means of time lengths," and he severely criticizes Beethoven for his structural reliance on harmony, which Cage sees as "the most intense lurching of the boat away from its natural even keel." Cage further identifies as noteworthy Satie's and Webern's "brevity and unpretentiousness of expression" and analyzes in terms of its phrase lengths Satie's *Choses vues à droite et à gauche (sans lunettes)* for violin and piano (1914). Internal evidence suggests that Cage's aversion to Beethoven may have been heightened by a discussion on the evening previous to his delivery of the lecture; but this possibility notwithstanding, given the largely Germanic Black Mountain faculty, it is unsurprising that Cage's words proved highly controversial, and the plan to publish the complete set of lectures was dropped. However, the general reaction to the Cage/Cunningham residency among staff and students was favorable: although they had agreed to appear on a non-fee basis, at their departure they were presented with a selection of gifts, including foodstuffs and artworks.[49]

While Cage's love of Satie might be attributable in part to the encouragement of Thomson, his knowledge of Webern is less easy to explain. Webern had been one of the two most successful Viennese pupils of Schoenberg, but his music was relatively unknown in America before the 1950s. One possible point of contact was the publication, in Cowell's *New Music Quarterly* in 1930, of the *Geistlicher Volkstext* opus 17, number 2 (1924–25); another was Lou Harrison, who (according to Revill, though this assertion is uncorroborated elsewhere) recommended that Cage investigate Webern's work.[50] By the time of the Black Mountain lecture, Cage was certainly familiar with both the opus 7 *Vier Stücke* (1910/14) for violin and piano (to which he refers) and the opus 5 *Fünf Sätze* for string quartet (1909), having heard the latter in a concert in approximately 1947.[51] But while Cage's interest in Satie continued throughout his life, his feelings for Webern appear to have diminished after the mid-1950s. Ironically, the seeds of this disinterest may have been sown during Cage's second visit to Europe in 1949.

Early that year—and largely, one suspects, as a result of the critical success of the *Sonatas and Interludes*—Cage was awarded a grant of one thousand dollars by the National Institute of Arts and Letters (NIAL) "for having extended the boundaries of musical art."[52] Unsurprisingly, given his previous sojourn there, Cage decided to spend most of his time in Paris (where Cunningham joined him in June), though he also visited Palermo. Equally unsurprisingly, one of Cage's principal interests in Paris was Satie: he took the opportunity to investigate his music and his writings and met with members of the Satie circle, including Darius Milhaud. Among the Satie scores that returned with Cage to New York were *Vexations* (1893) and some of the *Musique d'ameublement* (Furniture music; 1918/20/23); Cage arranged for *Vexations* to be published in *Contrepoints*, and both works resurfaced in his later life. An additional and unexpected pleasure that Cage experienced in Paris was the news that he was to be the recipient of an award of twenty-four hundred dollars from the Guggenheim Foundation. The offence caused to Peggy Guggenheim earlier in the decade had apparently been forgotten, and Cage was able to start work on a string quartet.

Through Thomson—who had "had a hand" in the NIAL and Guggenheim awards[53]—Cage had been supplied with introductions to two young French composers, Pierre Boulez and Serge Nigg. Boulez—who at this stage was among Webern's principal (albeit self-appointed) heirs—took immediately to Cage and opened up for him many opportunities in the French capital. Cage was admitted to the Boulez circle and introduced to composers including Pierre Schaeffer, the pioneer of *musique concrète* tape composition, and Boulez's teacher, Olivier Messiaen. Cage was already aware of Messiaen's music and had mentioned it in his 1946 article "The East in the West." His encounter with Schaeffer's work—in which recorded sounds are manipulated to produce the final piece—may have rekindled his earlier interests in electronic experimentation. Boulez also played for Cage his *Deuxième Sonate* and in turn listened to Cage perform the *Sonatas and Interludes*. He arranged for a prestigious private performance of the prepared-piano work, prefacing the event with a lecture in which he emphasized Cage's lineage as a former pupil of Schoenberg.

At this point, as is made clear in the voluminous correspondence that ensued once Cage had returned to New York, the two composers believed they had much in common, both technically and aesthetically. In Cage's case, the encounter with Boulez spurred him in the writing of words and music. The words were most immediately contained in two important texts, "Forerunners of Modern Music" and the "Lecture on Nothing." The former was published in New York, in the March 1949 issue of *The Tiger's Eye*, and later in *Contrepoints* (translated into French); the latter was delivered as a lecture at the Artists' Club in New York in 1950 and published in *Incontri Musicali* in 1959. Both pieces are included in *Silence*, and both feature unusual typographical layouts.[54]

"Forerunners of Modern Music" might, for two reasons, be thought of as revisiting the earlier text, "The Future of Music: Credo." First, its layout consists of italicized (rather than upper-case) headings (*The purpose of music; Definitions; Strategy;* etc.), which introduce short, though heavily footnoted, related discussions. The principal difference from the "Credo" lies in the nonlinearity of these headings (they do not in themselves form a continuous line of thought). Second, it too reads as a manifesto, and many of the issues it discusses are similar to those of the "Credo." Now, though, Cage includes numerous references to his recent philosophical and musical discoveries—Meister Eckhart, Sri Ramakrishna, Satie, Webern. The "Lecture on Nothing" is composed in a micro-macrocosmic structure of 7 : 6 : 14 : 14 : 7, the text being printed in four columns "to facilitate a rhythmic reading."[55] The lecture's individual units are separated by a punctuating sign—𝕸—and the large structural proportions by a double sign—𝕸𝕸. Cage further cued the structural divisions to his original live audience by such sentences as

Here we are now			at the	beginning	of the
ninth unit	of the	fourth large part	of this	talk.[56]	

As James Pritchett has argued, the "Lecture on Nothing" is "no longer just a conduit for information, but is both an explanation and a concrete demonstration of ideas. . . . This is the model that [Cage] was to follow increasingly in future years, becoming less and less interested in plain essaying, and more concerned with writing such musical lectures that would fill his need for poetry."[57] The "Lecture on Nothing" shares many ideas with "Forerunners of Modern Music," but, somewhat paradoxically given its layout and poetic style, it expresses them more clearly. Four of the lecture's five main sections are concerned respectively with form, structure, materials, and method; the fourth main section, functioning as a kind of interlude, is a meditation on stasis or, as Pritchett puts it, "a concrete demonstration of 'saying nothing.'"[58] The principal intention in the "Lecture on Nothing" is to exemplify the emptiness and the discipline inherent in durational structuring (i.e., micro-macrocosmic form); but it also makes evident the realization that had been emerging in Cage's music for some time that a durational structure need not present a coherent, linear argument but could rather contain a succession of syntactically unrelated objects, including silences. Furthermore, the lecture is also—especially in its third section, which deals with materials—unusually explicit in providing details of Cage's emerging technical and aesthetic concerns. Beginning with the confession

I remember loving   sound   before I ever   took a   music lesson[59]

it moves on to mention such early musical likes and dislikes as Grieg, Bach, and Brahms. After a discussion of modern music comes one of Cage's most famous remarks—

          I found that I   liked noises   even more than I
liked intervals.[60]

—which is in turn followed by a description of his use of sirens and of a coil of wire attached to a phonograph arm (as employed in the second and third *Imaginary Landscapes*).

Two other, related features of the "Lecture on Nothing" should be mentioned here. First, near the start of the lecture is another of Cage's most famous utterances:

                                        I have   nothing to say
          and I am   saying it   and that is
poetry   as I need it   .[61]

At the end of the lecture, Cage provides an "Afternote" describing the "question and answer" session that followed its original delivery; for this he had prepared, in advance, six answers that would be given whatever the questions. Both of these features, to a greater or lesser extent, indicate that by this point he had begun his investigation of Zen Buddhism, which was to become his dominant aesthetic and philosophical focus of the next decade or so. The "non-answers" are in particular reminiscent of the Zen *koan* or *mondo*.[62] Whether this suggests that Cage had already begun attending the series of lectures given at Columbia University by Daisetz Teitaro Suzuki is debatable, though: as David Patterson has shown, Cage's recollections concerning the dates of his attendance at those lectures are at odds with the facts.[63] Consequently, as Patterson has concluded (and contrary to the impression given by Cage in his writings and interviews), "[I]t is extremely difficult to gauge the proper weight that Suzuki is to be afforded in Cage's aesthetic development."[64]

Cage's frequent later allusions to Suzuki are a prime example of his tendency to name-drop: the Cage literary canon is littered with references to such luminaries as Schoenberg, Duchamp, Suzuki, Buckminster Fuller, Marshall McLuhan, and so on. As he most famously put it in a 1989 interview with William Duckworth, "I think I am actually an elitist. I always have been. I didn't study music with just anybody; I studied with Schoenberg. I didn't study Zen with just anybody; I studied with Suzuki. I've always gone, insofar as I could, to the president of the company."[65] Whether this desire to study with the principal authorities in given areas of inquiry is actually elitism, or is symptomatic rather of a keen wish to achieve vicarious celebrity, is a moot point; and one might also note that such apparent immodesty serves as a strong rejoinder to the more usual Cagean stance of (possibly self-serving or false) modesty and self-deprecation. Cage had been a bright but essentially lonely child, an outsider; now, as a brilliant but impoverished maverick composer, he was still to a considerable extent a loner, artistically situated well outside the mainstream musical establishment. In this context, it is no doubt significant that many of the historical figures Cage chose to champion or cite—from Meister Eckhart to Satie and (later) Henry David Thoreau—were also outsiders. Similarly significant is the way that Cage seized upon and promulgated a (somewhat dubious) remark attributed to Schoenberg: that Cage was "[n]ot a composer, but an inventor. Of genius."[66]

Such matters notwithstanding, the "Lecture on Nothing" clearly shows that by 1950, Cage's study of Oriental thought had already moved from South Asia (India) to East Asia (Japan). In parallel fashion, Cage's musical path was also moving even further from the emotion and determinacy of the 1930s and 1940s towards the acceptance, "giving up control," and eventual indeterminacy of the 1950s and beyond. In terms of his actual compositions, the work that demonstrates the commencement of this process, as well as showing the early results of his encounter with Boulez, is the *String Quartet in Four Parts* (1949–50). The work was commenced in Paris (though completed in New York) and develops several existing facets of Cage's compositional language. The piece is structured in micro-macrocosmic proportions of 2 ½ : 1 ½ :: 2 : 3 :: 6 : 5 :: ½ : 1 ½ (with successive pairs of proportional figures deployed in each of the four movements, making the third by far the longest) and is timbrally refined through the use of a gamut of sounds, intervals, and aggregates; this affords the work a limited but distinctly integrated sound world. These restrictions are amplified through the absence of vibrato and the specification of the strings to be played on: thus the gamut, in David Bernstein's word, becomes immobile.[67] This effect is further enhanced through Cage composing the piece as a quasi-monodic "melodic line without accompaniment."[68] Interestingly, in this context, the work is dedicated to Lou Harrison, a great lover of monody, though the vertical density of the outer movements somewhat contradicts this intention. Following on from *The Seasons*, the *String Quartet in Four Parts* is heavily influenced by Asian aesthetics: while the whole work (with the exception of the short final "Quodlibet") might be heard as a concrete example of "season[ing] and sober[ing] the mind, thus making it susceptible of divine influences, and elevating one's affections to goodness," the third movement also evokes the Zenlike stasis of the fourth section of the "Lecture on Nothing." A further link with Cage's 1947 ballet is found in the quartet's depiction of a seasonal progress: beginning with summer (in France), it gradually slows through fall (in America) to winter, before the celebration of the rebirth of spring in the sprightly finale. It is perhaps significant that although the quartet was begun in Paris, Cage "didn't have the courage" to show it to Boulez while he was there and later confessed that he was "terrified to show [him] this work."[69] The *String Quartet in Four Parts*, despite the rigor and apparent impersonality of its construction, is—in its sound and surface—a huge distance away from the contemporaneous music of Boulez.

The New York Schools

On January 17, 1950, Cage wrote Boulez a long letter in which he described the *First Construction (in Metal)* and mentioned that "Suzuki's works on Zen Buddhism are about to be published." Towards the end of the letter, he remarks that "[t]he great trouble with our life here is the absence of an intellectual life. No one has an idea. And should one by accident get one, no one would have the time to consider it."[70] That Cage could claim there was an "absence of an intellectual life" in New York at that time seems surprising and unjustified. He was surrounded by friends and colleagues who were—in various ways—working at the forefront of new ideas in the arts and with whom Cage must have had many stimulating conversations; this group would have included Henry Cowell, Merce Cunningham, Lou Harrison, and Virgil Thomson. Moreover, in the same letter he refers to recent contacts with Aaron Copland, Merton Brown, and the pianist William Masselos. Cage was also heavily involved with the contemporary art world: he had met Robert Rauschenberg two years previously at Black Mountain College; he was friendly with many of the abstract-expressionist artists collectively known as the New York School (including Mark Rothko, Willem de Kooning, and Philip Guston, as well as the sculptor Richard Lippold); and since at least 1949 he had been a member of the Artists' Club, which has been described as "'the primary arbiter of what would be called abstract expressionism.'"[71] It was at the Artists' Club during this period that Cage delivered three of his lectures, "Indian Sand Painting, or The Picture That Is Valid for One Day" (1949), the "Lecture on Nothing" (ca. 1949–50), and the "Lecture on Something" (1951). He was also an invited contributor to periodicals produced by other club members, including *The Tiger's Eye* and *Possibilities*.

Perhaps Cage's remark was ultimately prompted simply by his return to the routine of daily life in New York, following the excitement of his time in Paris. But even if one accepts his view of the "absence of an intellectual life," Cage's situation was about to change dramatically: only nine days after his letter to Boulez, Cage attended a Carnegie Hall concert at which Mitropoulos conducted Webern's Symphony, opus 21 (1927–28). Possibly as a result of the hostile audience reaction to the piece, and almost certainly having no wish to hear the Rachmaninov *Symphonic Dances*, opus 45, that was scheduled to complete the program, Cage left the auditorium after the Webern; in the lobby was another early departee, Morton Feldman (1926–87). "'I recognized [John], though we had never met, walked over and, as though I had known him all my life, said, "Wasn't that beautiful?" . . . We immediately made arrangements for me to visit him.'"[72] As a result of this meeting, Cage and Feldman spent a great deal of time together; their closeness was intensified when Feldman moved into another apartment in the "Bozza Mansion" (named after its landlord), where Cage was already a resident. Through Feldman, Cage became reacquainted with the pianist (and later composer) David Tudor (1926–96). Coincidentally, through another pianist, Cage's long-time friend Grete Sultan, the group was joined by Christian Wolff (born 1934), a high-school student who wished to study composition. The artistic vacuum that had supposedly existed in Cage's life prior to 1950 was consequently replaced by an invigorating new atmosphere in which "'[t]hings were really popping all the time. Ideas just flew back and forth between us, and in a sense we gave each other permission for the new music we were discovering.'"[73] Cage's assessment is supported by Feldman and Wolff, the latter having stated that "'[t]he people we were writing for were basically each other . . . until Earle [Brown] came along, [Feldman and I] were the two composers that [Cage] was the most interested in, because we were doing stuff that he had never seen before and that he happened to like. And there were new ideas floating around.'"[74]

Although the intellectual relationships among what has come to be known as the New York School of Composers were at this point intense, they were also somewhat haphazard. Given his relative youth, Wolff spent time with the others mostly during the afternoon and early evening. Cage and Feldman, meanwhile, often spent evenings together in the Cedar Tavern, where the talk was more about painting than music. Tudor's interactions with the group are less well documented, though Calvin Tomkins has opined that "Cage, Feldman, and Tudor met nearly every day . . . in Cage's Monroe Street apartment."[75] While the three composers composed, Tudor became their principal performer. He possessed a formidable technique and prepared himself for each new work with extraordinary thoroughness. For instance, having at Cage's instigation taken over from William Masselos responsibility for the first American performance of Boulez's *Deuxième Sonate*, he taught himself French in order to read in the original language the literature by Stéphane Mallarmé, René Char, and Antonin Artaud that had inspired Boulez's aesthetic. In later years, as John Holzaepfel has shown, Tudor frequently made extremely detailed performing versions of the indeterminate scores presented to him by the New York composers.

The works composed by Cage in the first two years of his association with Feldman, Tudor, and Wolff saw him, to a considerable degree, continuing along the lines suggested in the late 1940s. However, there is also a strong sense in which those works were encouraged in their boldness by the "permission" gained from his new associates, as well as by the concurrent exchanges with Boulez. Square-root form and the general idea of the gamut remain; but they are increasingly used in the generation of pieces that—in Henry Cowell's memorable phrase—appear to "'get rid of the glue so that the sounds [can] be themselves.'"[76] Using "little scraps of ideas that were left over from the *String Quartet*," Cage composed the *Six Melodies for Violin and Piano* (1950).[77] In *A Flower* (1950), the sound world of *The Wonderful Widow of Eighteen Springs* is recalled, albeit via a structure in which two micro-macrocosmic layers are superimposed. And *Works of Calder* (1950), a score for a film by Herbert Matter, brings together prepared piano and taped sounds that originated in a desire "to write without musical ideas (unrelated sounds)," though the end result seems to have been more pragmatic.[78] (Interestingly, although Cage accepted this film commission, he passed to Feldman the opportunity the following year to write the soundtrack for a documentary about Jackson Pollock. Cage may have been too busy; but he may also have been influenced by the character of the film's intended subject, one of the few individuals for whom Cage ever expressed a dislike.)

Following the *String Quartet in Four Parts*, most of Cage's energy was expended on three major projects—the *Sixteen Dances* (1950–51), the *Concerto for Prepared*

Piano and Orchestra (1950–51), and the *Music of Changes* (1951)—which saw him finally reject the remnants of subjective choice in favor of supposedly objective chance. The compositional history of the first two of these works is interwoven—the final third movement of the concerto was written after the completion of the *Sixteen Dances*. Cage saw the concerto's first movement as "a drama based upon the opposition of the prepared piano and the orchestra."[79] Accordingly, the solo part was freely composed, while the orchestral part was based in systematic procedures: a gamut of single sounds, intervals, and aggregates was arranged into a 14 x 16–cell grid. Each horizontal row was associated with a specific instrument, and Cage moved around the grid as if it were a checker board.[80] In the second movement, a grid was also used for the piano: thus the sense of drama and opposition is lessened, and the material for the soloist and accompanying ensemble accordingly moves "closer to a 'chance' or if you like an un-aesthetic choice."[81] The moves about the grid were now made via a series of concentric circles. While Cage maintained micro-macrocosmic rhythmic structure here, representing "the 'espace sonore' in which [each] of these sounds may exist and change," he saw composition increasingly as becoming the "throwing [of] sound into silence."[82]

At this point, work on the *Concerto for Prepared Piano and Orchestra* was set aside, as Cage took up a new commission from Cunningham that resulted in the *Sixteen Dances* for flute, trumpet, violin, cello, piano, and percussion. (With the exception of the percussion, this instrumentation is identical to that of Feldman's *Projection 2*, completed on January 3, 1951.) Like the *Sonatas and Interludes*, *The Seasons*, and the *String Quartet in Four Parts*, the *Sixteen Dances* were influenced by Cage's South Asian studies: each of the odd-numbered movements is associated with one of the permanent emotions of Indian tradition and is followed by an interlude; the final movement represents tranquility.[83] Like the concerto, the musical material of the dances is derived from a grid, this time 8 x 8; here, though, the initial gamut of sounds was systematically replaced, and the moves about the grid were determined by a magic square.[84] A particular feature of the *Sixteen Dances*, further recalling the *Two Pieces for Piano* and *The Seasons*, is their use of extended silences.

By the time Cage returned to the *Concerto for Prepared Piano and Orchestra*, Wolff—in return for his composition lessons—had presented Cage with an English translation of the ancient Chinese oracular *I Ching* (Book of Changes), which had been published by Wolff's father in 1950. Although Lou Harrison had previously introduced Cage to the *I Ching*, at that stage it had held no interest for him. But now, on opening the book Cage was struck by the correlation between its contents and the grids he had been using: by a remarkable coincidence, the *I*

Ching is organized into sixty-four (8 x 8) hexagrams (six-line figures). Cage "imme-diately saw that the [*I Ching's*] chart was better than the Magic Square."[85] Thus, in the concerto's third movement, Cage "adapted the *I Ching* to merge the two charts used in the second movement into a single chart."[86] As a result, Cage took his final step away from choice and into the world of chance, where, as James Pritchett memorably puts it, "each sound emerges of itself from the empty space of the rhythmic structure."[87]

The full implications of this decisive move were realized in Cage's next work, the quadripartite *Music of Changes*. Like the *Concerto for Prepared Piano and Orchestra*, it continues to use micro-macrocosmic structuring; but whereas the concerto's solo part was written for an elaborately prepared instrument, here the piano is unaltered (though Cage does require that some sounds are produced away from the keyboard, notably on the strings and on the casing). The compositional processes employed in the *Music of Changes*—in order that the sounds might be themselves or (in Zen terms) be unimpeded and interpenetrating[88]—were extraordinarily complex and were significantly influenced by the virtuosity of David Tudor. Sixty-four-cell (8 x 8) charts, or grids, were prepared for all aspects of the music—sonority, duration, and dynamics—and for each notated gesture it was consequently necessary for Cage to consult the *I Ching*, by thrice tossing coins or yarrow sticks to identify a particular hexagram. The charts of sonori-ties contained equal amounts of sound and silence; those for duration contained sixty-four separate values, some of which were highly irrational; and the dynamic charts were constructed to allow the continuation of existing dynamics as well as the introduction of new ones. Beyond this, the structural proportions of the work are 29 ⅝ x 29 ⅝ (divided as 3 : 5 : 6 ¾ : 6 ¾ : 5 : 3 ⅛), the tempo is variable, and the score is notated according to a "scale" of quarter-note = 2 ½ cm.[89]

Lest it be surmised that such chance-based complexities led to musical chaos, three related points should be made: first and foremost, Cage approached each of his chance-derived works with a clear aural result in mind. Whether it be the deliberately pointillistic, Webernesque *Music of Changes*, the "wrong-note Satie" of *Cheap Imitation* (1969), or the Joycean collage of *Roaratorio* (1979), the chance procedures adopted by Cage were devised in pursuit of a particular musical goal; chance freed him from decision making at the microcosmic but assuredly *not* the macrocosmic level. As Virgil Thomson pointed out in a review of *Music of Changes*, "'The sounds of it, many of them complex, are carefully chosen, invented by him . . . and their composition in time is no less carefully worked out.'"[90] Second, the sound world of *Music of Changes* is not dissimilar to that of a work that is in many ways its close cousin (albeit one created via a diametrically opposed method, integral serialism), Boulez's contemporaneous first book of *Structures* (1952). And third, despite its compositional complexities, the actual score of the *Music of Changes* (unlike those of Cage's percussion and prepared-piano pieces) looks very much like the way it sounds, with clustered collections of notes frequently surrounded by empty space.

Cage completed *Music of Changes* in December 1951, less than a month before Tudor gave its first performance at New York's Cherry Lane Theater. He had described the work's compositional processes in detail to Boulez in a letter dated May 22, 1951; in his reply, Boulez wrote that he "found it incredibly interesting" and that "we are at the same stage of research."[91] But at the end of the year, he qualified his enthusiasm: "Everything you say about the tables of sounds, durations, amplitudes, used in your Music of Changes is . . . along exactly the same lines as I am working at the moment. . . . The only thing, forgive me, which I am not happy with, is the method of absolute chance (*by tossing the coins*). On the contrary, I believe that chance must be extremely controlled."[92] This letter also continued the criticisms of Feldman's music that Boulez had already aired in May and August. Thus, by the time that he arrived in New York in November 1952 (he was music director of the visiting Renaud-Barrault theater troupe), his friendship with Cage, though not yet soured, had already begun to curdle.

During Boulez's time in New York (spent in Cage's apartment, which Cage loaned to him), two further areas of difficulty emerged. First, until this point Boulez had shared Cage's dislike of Stravinsky's music. In the 1930s, Cage—as a Schoenberg pupil—had given a Los Angeles impresario short shrift over his description of Stravinsky as "the World's Greatest Living Composer."[93] In late 1951, Boulez had written to Cage: "'Have you heard Rake's progress? What ugliness!'"[94] Yet, according to Virgil Thomson, when Boulez and Stravinsky met at Thomson's home, they "'hit like comets. . . . Stravinsky needed the support of the young, while Boulez was pleased to have Papa's blessing.'"[95] It was to be some years before Cage made *his* peace with Stravinsky, rather bizarrely in 1966 after a performance of *The Soldier's Tale* in which Cage was cast as the Devil. Second, a series of petty issues upset Cage: "'Once, on our way back from Cape Cod, we ran out of gas. Pierre thought that was inelegant. I also remember a diner in Providence. Pierre was indignant over the service and the food, and I believe that he required us to leave. I was always frightened by his superior taste. He was always uncompromising. Things had to be exactly where they should be.'"[96] Although a number of cordial letters were exchanged in the fifteen months following Boulez's return to France, there had clearly been a fundamental change in the relationship. Subsequently, Boulez's increasingly combative nature (he had had recent battles with Nicolas Nabokov and Pierre Schaeffer, following on from an earlier rift with René Leibowitz) and his integration into the mainstream post-Webernian European avant-garde ensured that he avoided Cage and Tudor completely during their continental tour in the fall of 1954. By this time, he no doubt concurred with Heinrich Strobel's alleged description of their activities as "'poor Dada.'"[97]

If Cage's friendship with Boulez waxed and waned during these years, his closeness with the members of the New York School intensified and was of significant mutual benefit. Earlier, reference was made to the feeling shared by Cage, Feldman, and Wolff that they "gave each other permission" for the new music they were discovering. In Cage's case, this related directly to the *Music of Changes*. On seeing the *I Ching*'s sixty-four-hexagram chart, he immediately sketched out the whole procedure for the work: "'I ran over to show the plan to Morty Feldman, who had taken a studio in the same building, and I can still remember him saying, "You've hit it!"'"[98] Similarly, for Feldman the cross-influence led to his invention of graphic notation: "'Feldman left the room one evening, in the midst of a long conversation, and returned later with a composition on graph paper.'"[99] The work in question was *Projection 1* (1950) for solo cello, which was completed before Cage had even commenced the precisely notated (and therefore, in Feldman's term, "photographically still") *Music of Changes*.

That Cage was deeply impressed by his colleagues' work is clearly evident from the text of the "Lecture on Something," which is concerned with topics that follow from those discussed in the "Lecture on Nothing" and specific matters related to Feldman and his music. But whereas—as James Pritchett puts it—"the 'Lecture on Nothing' is all-negating, [the] 'Lecture on Something' is all-affirming":[100]

			To accept		whatever comes
		re-	gardless	of the	consequences
	is to be		unafraid		or
		to be	full	of that	love which
	comes from	a	sense of at-one-ness		with whatever[101]

The concrete, musical evidence of Cage deriving inspiration from his colleagues is apparent in the works he produced during 1952, his compositional *annus mirabilis*. The processes used in writing the *Music of Changes* were clearly laborious, but Cage continued to employ them in the works that immediately succeeded it. These include *Two Pastorales* (1951–52) for prepared piano and three pieces for piano: *Seven Haiku* (1951–52), *Waiting* (1952), and *For MC and DT* (1952).

More related to the notion of "accepting whatever comes" is *Imaginary Land-scape No. 4* (1951) for twelve radios, each operated by two performers, in which Cage specifies precisely both volume and frequency (that is, the frequencies to which each radio should be tuned). What he cannot specify, of course, are the sounds (or lack of them) that will result. Cage certainly intended that the work be quiet, but the lateness of the hour at its first performance resulted in it becoming almost inaudible, as there were few stations broadcasting at that time. This led to considerable criticism, not least from Virgil Thomson, who apparently later told Cage that he "'had better not perform a piece like that before a paying public.'"[102] Sadly, this exchange finally ended his friendship with Thomson, which had already been unsettled by Cage's "definitely unfriendly" contributions to a book on the older composer.[103]

A transitional work in which Cage begins to move toward nontraditional (Feldman-influenced) notation is the tape piece *Williams Mix* (1952). Written in eight layers (for either eight single-track or four two-track tape recorders), the score resembles a dressmaker's pattern, from which the tapes were cut to size and shape.[104] The huge range of source sounds—whether of city, country, or music (electronic, conventional, or vocal)—was collected by Cage, Tudor, and Louis and Bebe Barron. Funding for the project (which amounted to five thousand dollars) was provided by a former Black Mountain College student, Paul Williams—hence the work's title—and the tape cutting was carried out by Cage, Tudor, the Barrons, and a new associate, Earle Brown (1926–2002). Brown and his wife, the dancer Carolyn Brown, had met Cage and Cunningham in Denver during 1951. The following year, they moved to New York, where Earle joined Cage's "Project for Magnetic Tape" team and Carolyn began a long association with Cunningham's dance company. The work on *Williams Mix*—like that of *Music of Changes*—proved so time-consuming that only the first section of the piece, lasting four and a half minutes, was completed. However, the "Project for Magnetic Tape" also resulted in several other pieces—including Brown's *Octet I* (1952–53), Wolff's *For Magnetic Tape* (1952), and the Barrons' *For an Electronic Nervous System* (1954)—that were among the first such works composed in the United States.

During the remainder of 1952, Cage experimented with a variety of unconventional notations, which were to a considerable degree influenced by the work of Feldman and, to a lesser extent, Brown.[105] His first truly graphic score, written in January for a dance by Jean Erdman, was *Imaginary Landscape No. 5*, for any forty-two phonograph records recorded onto tape. In its layout, the work is remarkably similar to many of Feldman's graphs. Nine months later, in *Music for*

Carillon No. 1, Cage produced a kind of blueprint for a piece: each of the score's pages has two systems, each lasting ten seconds; horizontal space represents time, and vertical space represents relative pitch. The score can either be played verbatim—in which case it becomes partly indeterminate of its performance—or transcribed into more conventional notation. This latter possibility was taken up by Cage himself, who later published space-time versions of the piece for two-octave and three-octave carillons. The compositional process employed in making the original graphic score was much simpler than that of *Music of Changes* and *Williams Mix:* templates were created by arbitrarily folding pieces of paper and then making holes at the intersections of the folds. The templates were superimposed onto graph paper, and the holes drawn through, resulting in tiny dots (equating to notes) on the graph; durations were not specified.[106] Simpler still was the process adopted in the *Music for Piano* series, commenced in December 1952 and eventually completed a decade later with the unpublished *Music for Piano 85*. Here, Cage identified imperfections in the manuscript paper and marked them; the *I Ching* was used to determine the number of markings per page, as well as clefs, and so on. The exact procedures employed for one (1955) series of these pieces is given in Cage's article "To Describe the Process of Composition Used in *Music for Piano 21–52*."[107]

The most extreme example of Cage's notational innovations of 1952 is found in *Water Music* (spring 1952), the score of which, in much reduced form, is shown on page 57. Consisting of a large (55" x 34") sheet of musical and textual instructions, the score is suspended or otherwise positioned in view not only of its performer but also the audience. In addition to a partly prepared piano, the soloist requires a variety of other objects, including whistles, playing cards, a radio, and water. *Water Music* is a hybrid work in at least two ways: first, although it still makes use of Cage's earlier chart techniques, metrical time is replaced by clock time. Second, the piece is as much theatrical as purely musical; in this, it inaugurated a series of similarly cross-disciplinary pieces that emerged from Cage's pen over the next several decades.

Distinct parallels can also be drawn between Cage's music of this period and the contemporaneous work of Robert Rauschenberg (a member of the *other* New York School), with which Cage was well acquainted. In the summer of 1950, Rauschenberg and his then wife, Sue Weil, had experimented with "blueprint paper, placing various objects on sheets of it and exposing them to sunlight."[108]

Opposite: John Cage, Water Music. *Edition Peters No. 6770.* © 1960 *Henmar Press Inc., New York. Used by permission of Peters Edition Limited, London.*

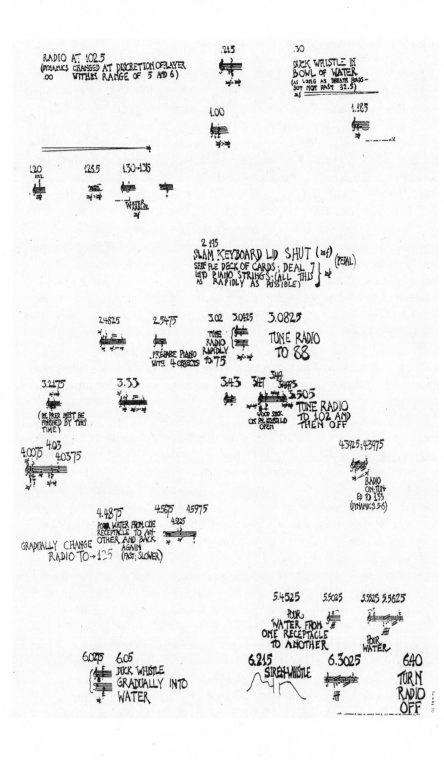

During the winter of 1950–51, his work became "abstract with figurative signs and symbols, such as black arrows and hands and flowerlike sequences of forms." Subsequently, Rauschenberg worked with dirt, which he rubbed into white pigment, and red lead. These experiments led directly to a series of all-white and all-black paintings, which were of major importance to two of Cage's works. First, the white canvasses—suspended from the ceiling and used as a backdrop for slides and a film by Nicholas Cernovitch—were one element in the infamous *Black Mountain Piece* (1952). Despite his earlier differences with the college faculty, Cage had been invited back to Black Mountain College in the summer of 1952 by Lou Harrison. At Black Mountain, Cage organized what has become known as the first "happening," in which—in the spirit of "accepting whatever comes"—a number of independent activities took place simultaneously. Within a predetermined time frame, each performer "could fill their 'compartments' with whatever materials they chose."[109] Cage, standing on a ladder, read his forty-five-minute "Juilliard Lecture" (1952; its first rendition had been juxtaposed with a piano recital by Tudor); Mary Caroline Richards and Charles Olson read poetry from another ladder; Rauschenberg played records on an Edison phonograph; Tudor played the piano; and Cunningham "danced down the aisles followed by a dog." The audience of students and staff sat "in a square broken into four triangles whose apexes merged toward the center."[110]

The second work to be influenced by Rauschenberg's all-white and all-black paintings was the "silent" piece, *4' 33"* (1952), which is without doubt Cage's best-known and least-understood composition. It stands out as his major aesthetic statement and the focus of much uncomprehending criticism, as well as being the butt of countless jokes. In fact, *4' 33"* had a surprisingly long gestation. As early as 1948, in "A Composer's Confessions," Cage had spoken of his desire "to compose a piece of uninterrupted silence and sell it to Muzak Co. It will be 3 or 4 ½ minutes long—those being the standard lengths of 'canned' music—and its title will be *Silent Prayer*. It will open with a single idea which I will attempt to make as seductive as the color and shape and fragrance of a flower. The ending will approach imperceptibility."[111] This idea lay dormant, however, until 1952, when two events conspired in its completion. First, Cage encountered Rauschenberg's all-black and all-white paintings; previously, he had been afraid "that my making a piece that had no sounds in it would appear as if I were making a joke. In fact, I probably worked longer on my 'silent' piece than I worked on any other . . . what pushed me into it was not guts but the example of Robert Rauschenberg. When I saw those [paintings], I said 'Oh yes, I must; otherwise I'm lagging, otherwise music is lagging.'"[112] Or, more succinctly, "The white paintings came first; my silent piece came later."[113] Second, at some point in 1952 Cage visited an anechoic chamber at Harvard University. Expecting to experience absolute silence, Cage was surprised to hear two sounds, one high, the other low; he described them to the engineer, who informed him that the first was his nervous system, the second the circulation of his blood. Cage had "honestly and naively thought that some actual silence existed. . . . When I went into that sound-proof room, I really expected to hear nothing."[114] Now he had to change his opinion and, for perhaps the first time, to follow through to its conclusion the logic of accepting "whatever comes regardless of the consequences"—which in this case meant accepting, and indeed highlighting, the plethora of ambient unintended sounds that constantly surround us. As Cage wrote in the "Juilliard Lecture":

| | Not one sound | fears | the silence that ex- | tinguishes it. | And |
| no silence exists | that is not | | pregnant | with | sound.[115] |

Or, as he put it in "Experimental Music" (1957), "There is no such thing as an empty space or an empty time. There will always be something to see, something to hear. In fact, try as we may to make a silence, we cannot."[116]

The score of *4′33″* exists in several versions; moreover, the work can in fact be of any length and be performed by any instrument(s). But its effect has always been the same: of shock for unprepared listeners and—one hopes—of pleasure for the remainder. It was certainly the former reaction that predominated at the work's premiere, in Woodstock, N.Y., on August 29, 1952. David Tudor walked to the piano, closed the keyboard lid, and began the first, thirty-second-long movement. Breaks between the movements (the second lasted 2′ 23″, the third 1′ 40″) were indicated by the lid being opened and then reclosed. Cage said that he "knew that it would be taken as a joke and a renunciation of work" but nevertheless "wanted my work to be free of my own likes and dislikes, because I think music should be free of the feelings and ideas of the composer. I have felt and hoped to have led other people to feel that the sounds of their environment constitute a music which is more interesting than the music which they would hear if they went into a concert hall."[117]

In fact, there was plenty to listen to that evening in Woodstock: "You could hear the wind stirring outside during the first movement. During the second, raindrops began patterning the roof." But "[d]uring the third the people themselves made all kinds of interesting sounds as they talked or walked out."[118] Unlike Cage himself—for whom the work remained his favorite—the audience had not followed the very particular aesthetic, philosophical, and musical path that, during the late 1940s and early 1950s, led to the iconoclasm of *4′33″*; indeed, as a result of writing the piece, Cage "had friends whose friendship [he] valued and whose friendship [he] lost."[119] And notwithstanding the forty-dollar weekly stipend he had received during the compositional period of *Williams Mix*, Cage was still—a decade after his arrival in New York—effectively penniless. Crucially, however, he had now found, in the words of Howard Gardner, "a set of peers"—Brown, Cunningham, Feldman, Tudor, and Wolff—"who [shared] the same interests" and with whom he could "explore the terrain of [his] domain . . . organizing institutions, issuing manifestos, and stimulating one another to new heights."[120]

3 | Stony Point, 1954–70

THE ARTISTIC AND AESTHETIC friendships among the members of the New York School of Composers lasted through the remainder of their lives, but the closeness and intensity of their relationships, as well as their physical proximity to each other, were much shorter-lived. Cage, Feldman, Tudor, and Wolff became acquainted during the early months of 1950 and over the next few years spent a great deal of time together. In 1952, Earle Brown joined them, though this was to some extent as much a negative as a positive event: from the start, Feldman had been almost obsessively protective of the initial group's integrity. According to Cage, in 1950 and 1951, "There were other people who wanted to enter the group and enjoy the exchange of ideas and so forth. . . . Morty refused to let that happen. He insisted upon its being a closed group."[1] Among those excluded were Philip Corner, Malcolm Goldstein, and James Tenney. On Brown's arrival, Feldman appeared to be friendly; but underneath he was furious, so that "the closeness that [Cage] had had with Morty and David and Christian was disrupted."[2] The spark that lit the tinder was a discussion concerning Boulez, who (unbeknownst to Brown) had already made disparaging remarks about the work of Feldman and Wolff. According to David Revill, Cage, Feldman, and the Browns dropped into a diner. "Feldman criticized Boulez and his penchant for mathematics. . . . Brown defended the Frenchman, partly because of his own involvement with mathematics, as a scientist and an advocate of Schillinger techniques."[3] Feldman took Brown's comments as a personal attack and refused to acknowledge him for several years thereafter.

A second major factor contributing to the waning of the group's intensity was that of changing locations. In the summer of 1950, activities had been firmly centered on Bozza Mansion: Cage and Feldman were living there, while Wolff (and to a lesser extent Tudor) were frequent—sometimes daily—visitors. However, in the late summer of 1951 Wolff began his studies at Harvard; at some point in 1952, Feldman appears to have moved to the Washington Square area; and the Browns, on their arrival in New York, also settled in Greenwich Village. The final blow came in 1953, when Cage and his Bozza Mansion neighbors were served with notice to vacate, as the building was to be demolished prior to redevelopment. Cage moved in with Cunningham on East Seventeenth Street, but in August 1954, he—along with Tudor, Mary Caroline Richards, and David and Karen Weinrib—decamped to an artistic community founded by Paul Williams and his wife, a seventy-five-minute drive from New York City. With its members now located at various points between Cambridge, Massachusetts, and Lower Manhattan—and with two of them not even on speaking terms—the New York School, as a living entity, had effectively come to an end. To partly misappropriate a remark of Cage's, "We loved one another very much, but each life had gone in its own direction."[4]

My Cottage Becomes a Universe

Cage's new home was in the Hudson Valley, at Stony Point in Rockland County. The contrast with Bozza Mansion could not have been greater. From his top-floor apartment at the intersection of Monroe and Grand Streets, Cage had been able to "look up to 59th Street and . . . down to the Statue of Liberty, and I was spoiled by this involvement with the sky and air and water and so forth."[5] Until now, Cage had been fundamentally a child of the city—whether Los Angeles, Seattle, Chicago, or New York—and these environments had provided him with a multiplicity of artistic stimuli and a surprising degree of privacy and quietude. Having now, like Lou Harrison four years earlier, exchanged urban frenzy for rural tranquility, Cage suddenly found himself "living in small quarters with four other people, and I was not used to such a lack of privacy, so I took to walking in the woods. . . . [I]n Stony Point . . . I discovered that I was starved for nature."[6] Cage's initial accommodations were in the attic of a farmhouse; the cockroaches of New York were replaced by a colony of wasps, and "my whole [previously hostile] attitude towards insects changed."[7]

John Cage, seated on the wall that he built at his home in Stony Point, New York, ca. 1954–55. Photograph by David Gahr. Used by permission of the John Cage Trust.

Cage's woodland walks introduced him to fungi, the bright colors of which caught his eye. During the Depression, at Carmel, he had lived "for a week on nothing but mushrooms"; now he "decided to spend enough time to learn something about them."[8] The obsessiveness that, in Paris in 1930, had led to him studying Gothic balustrades in the Bibliothèque Mazarine now saw him become a collector of fungi and books about them. His three-hundred-volume mycological library, amassed over the next decade, was eventually donated to the University of California at Santa Cruz. His interest spawned a class in mushroom identification at New York's New School for Social Research, which in turn led to the founding of the New York Mycological Society. Cage became such an expert on fungi that he wrote a number of mycological texts, supplied mushrooms to some of New York's finest restaurants via the entrepreneur Emile d'Antonio, and even won an Italian quiz show on the subject.

Given Cage's continuing studies of Asian aesthetics and philosophy, it is interesting to contextualize his experiences of the next fifteen years at Stony Point through a poem by the Chinese writer Lu Yun (262–303):

THE VALLEY WIND

Living in retirement beyond the World,
Silently enjoying isolation,
I pull the rope of my door tighter
And stuff my window with roots and ferns.
My spirit is tuned to the Spring-season:
At the fall of the year there is autumn in my heart.
Thus imitating cosmic changes,
My cottage becomes a Universe.[9]

While the changes that Cage experienced in his life and work during the Stony Point period were hardly cosmic, they were certainly significant. Paradoxically, while much of the time he had spent in urban centers had been artistically frustrating and at times lonely, providing few opportunities for work elsewhere, from 1954 onwards—removed to the physical isolation of Stony Point—invitations began to flood in, whether to festivals in Europe or residencies in American universities and colleges. Similarly, his work began to reach a wider public, through his signing in 1961 of an exclusive publishing contract with the Henmar Press (part of the C. F. Peters Corporation) and the appearance the same year of his first (and most influential) collection of writings, *Silence*. On another front, one of the original attractions of moving to Stony Point was Paul Williams's intention that it would serve as a base for Cage's long-wished-for Center for Experimental Music. Although ultimately nothing came of this, an important aspect of Cage's work over the next decade was its increasing interaction with electronic media. Many of these projects were brought to fruition elsewhere, but there is a distinct sense in which the particular ambience of Cage's country cottage may have encouraged him in "reaching out," literally and metaphorically, via electricity to the universe beyond.[10]

Finally, as Cage attuned himself to nature, his new domicile further drew him to the surrounding sonic environment. The unintended sounds first foregrounded in *4′ 33″* now became the *musique d'ameublement* of his home. In 1965, Ninette Lyon wrote of "'the only melodies in [the] sparsely furnished two-room cabin [being] the creaking of a big white hammock, [and] the muffled sound of bare feet on cocoa matting.'"[11] And Cage himself, a little more flippantly, spoke in 1954 of spending "many pleasant hours in the woods conducting performances of my silent piece, transcriptions, that is, for an audience of myself. . . . At one performance, I passed the first movement by attempting the identification of a mushroom. . . .

The second movement was extremely dramatic, beginning with the sounds of a buck and a doe leaping up to within ten feet of my rocky podium."[12]

Prospection and Retrospection

Once settled at Stony Point, Cage initially continued the work that had occupied him in New York. The *Music for Piano* series had by now reached number *20* (completed in 1953) and was subsequently expanded to include numbers *21–52* (1955), *53–68*, and *69–84* (both 1956). Similarly, *Music for Carillon No. 1* (1952) was joined by two further pieces in 1954. The major project that occupied Cage through 1956, however, was the uncompleted series, commenced in 1953, which he referred to privately as "The Ten Thousand Things." Just as the various items in the *Music for Piano* series may be played simultaneously, or overlapped, so may the constituent parts of "The Ten Thousand Things," whose collective title refers to the number associated with infinity in Chinese Taoism and Buddhism.

In one of his last letters to Boulez, dated May 1, 1953, Cage mentioned that "from time to time ideas [come] for my next work which as I see it will be a large work which will always be in progress and will never be finished; at the same time any part of it will be able to be performed once I have begun. It will include tape and any other time actions, not excluding violins and whatever else I put my attention to."[13] All of the works in the "Ten Thousand Things" series share a structure in thirteen parts, with the proportions 3 : 7 : 2 : 5 : 11 : 14 : 7 : 6 : 1 : 15 : 11 : 3 : 15, which together total 100; at the macrocosmic level, this yields an overall length of 100^2 = 10,000. In fact, none of the works in the series is as long as one hundred units; rather, each work consists of one or more conjoined, contiguous parts drawn from the "master" set of thirteen (e.g., 3 : 7 : 2 : 5 : 11). These, as well as many other complexities associated with "The Ten Thousand Things," are explained by James Pritchett in *The Music of John Cage*.[14]

The first works of the series to be written were a set of six brief string pieces— *57 ½"*, *1′ 5 ½"*, *1′ 1 ½"*, *1′ 18"*, *1′ 14"*, and *59 ½"* (all 1953)—the first five of which were later incorporated into the longer *26′ 1.1499″ for a string player* (1953–55). These titles, representing the works' durations, are typical of the series; typical too is their notation, which, rather than emphasizing exact pitches, describes bands of activity. Here, four of the bands represent the four strings of the instrument; the remaining two respectively represent bowing pressure and noises of any type. Duration is notated similarly to that of the *Music of Changes*, with two centimeters equaling one beat; the tempo varies with each phrase. Instead of using a chart system for the gamut of available sounds (as in the *Concerto for Pre-*

pared Piano and Orchestra), Cage employed a variant of the point-drawing system. These basic compositional practices were developed during the writing of later pieces in the series: *34′ 46.776″ for a pianist* and *31′ 57.9864″ for a pianist* (both 1954) are for prepared piano. While the list of preparations details the strings to be prepared and the materials to be used in preparation, the placement of the materials is not; this allows considerable flexibility and draws the performer into the compositional and creative process. The notation is on staves, which are juxtaposed with bands describing the various factors (such as force of attack) that influence dynamics; duration is now notated in clock time. *27′ 10.554″ for a percussionist* (1956) features lines rather than bands, these representing the primary materials—metal, wood, skin, and "all others"—used in the construction of the instruments (which are selected by the performer rather than being specified by the composer). Duration is again shown chronometrically, and amplitude by the vertical position of the note heads in relation to the four lines.

Each of these works may be played as a solo or combined with one or more of the other pieces in the "Ten Thousand Things" series. In the fall of 1954, Cage and Tudor undertook a European tour, as part of which they gave a simultaneous performance of shortened versions of *34′ 46.776″* and *31′ 57.9864″* at the Donaueschinger Musiktage.[15] Mainly through the earlier advocacy of Boulez, the European avant-garde was aware of Cage's music for prepared piano, notably the *Sonatas and Interludes*. However, the new works—lacking the lyricism and rhythmic conventionality of the older pieces—came as something of a shock to the audience and were greeted with hostility. Boulez—whose *Le marteau sans maître* had been intended for the festival but was not performed there—avoided Donaueschingen that year, and the festival's director, Heinrich Strobel, described the Cage-Tudor performance (which also included *Water Music*) to him as "poor Dada."[16]

In addition to the engagement at Donaueschingen, Cage and Tudor performed in Cologne, Paris, Brussels, Stockholm, Zurich, Milan, and London.[17] A further event in London, the Composers' Concourse, saw Cage deliver an invited speech, "45′ for a Speaker," which—like the "Lecture on Nothing" and "Lecture on Something"—is "both an explanation and a concrete demonstration of ideas."[18] As might be surmised from its title, the speech was putatively part of the "Ten Thousand Things" series: Cage had originally intended to use the same structure as that of *34′ 46.776″*. Chance operations had given him a length of 39′ 16.95″, but this proved unfeasibly short in performance, so he allowed two seconds for each line of text, resulting in an overall duration of forty-five minutes. The text was composed during the European tour, and like *34′ 46.776″*, it incorporates extraneous sounds and actions including, in this case, snoring, hissing, slapping the table, and lighting a match. In the printed version of the lecture, relative vocal volume is notated via the typeface, and time is indicated chronometrically (though there seems to be an irrationality in its layout, as the following extract demonstrates: there are six, rather than the expected five, lines in each ten-second unit). The actual content of the lecture was a patchwork of extracts woven from Cage's earlier writings, to which was added some new material. Decisions concerning the nature of the material were made by answering a series of questions ("Is there speech or silence? And for how long? If speech, is it old material or new?" and so on) through chance operations. Some sense of the intentional discontinuity that results may be gleaned from the opening thirty seconds, which are recycled from two passages in the "Juilliard Lecture."[19]

0' 00"	"Lo and behold the horse turns into
	a prince, who, except for the
	acquiescence of the hero
	would have had to remain a
	miserable shaggy nag."
10"	I have noticed something else about
	Christian Wolff's music. All you can
	do is
	suddenly listen
	in the same way
	that, when you catch cold,
20"	all you can do is
	suddenly
	sneeze.
	Unfortunately —
	European harmony.

30"

This passage is followed by a twenty-second silence, after which Cage continues with an extract from the "Lecture on Nothing."[20]

Cage completed two more pieces in the period through 1956; both feature radios and demonstrate further his interests in indeterminacy and "accepting whatever comes." *Speech 1955*, for five radios and a newsreader, has six individual parts but no score. As in *Imaginary Landscape No. 4*, "[S]pecific time indications are given and [there are] graphic suggestions for the playing of [the] radios."[21] *Radio Music* (1956) was written for one to eight radios: its indeterminacy is heightened

through "the length of each [of its four] section[s being] determined by the performer . . . stop-watches are used in performance."[22] However, as a condescension
to "the people who were disturbed over the *Imaginary Landscape No. 4* because it
was so quiet," maximum volume is maintained throughout.[23]

By 1957, Cage's activities were becoming more numerous. He was arrang-
ing occasional concerts in New York and elsewhere—mostly featuring his own
music and that of his associates—and was increasingly involved in Cunningham's
dance company in his role as its music director. Following the example of Henry
Cowell, he had begun to teach at the New School for Social Research. His students in the Composition of Experimental Music class over the next few years
included George Brecht, Dick Higgins, Toshi Ichiyanagi, Allan Kaprow, and
Jackson MacLow. The demands of his schedule were the principal reason why
Cage became protective of the time that remained for composition: thus when
Rauschenberg, d'Antonio, and a new artist friend, Jasper Johns (born 1930)—
whom Cage had met around 1954—suggested a major retrospective concert of
his work, Cage was "flattered but reluctant to pursue it."[24] That the event actually took place, on May 15, 1958, was almost entirely due to the efforts of Tudor
(who selected the program), d'Antonio, Johns, and Rauschenberg (these last three
teaming up to form "Impresarios Inc.").

The Twenty-Five-Year Retrospective Concert, as it was billed, was given in
New York's Town Hall and, according to Calvin Tomkins, "the entire New York
avant-garde turned out . . . in a demonstration of artistic solidarity seldom dupli-
cated before or since."[25] The works performed at the event covered the whole
range of Cage's oeuvre to that point, starting with the *Six Short Inventions* of 1933
(in a new arrangement for seven instruments). The later 1930s were represented
by two ensemble pieces—the *First Construction (in Metal)* and *Imaginary Landscape
No. 1*—and the earlier 1940s by two vocal works, *The Wonderful Widow of Eighteen Springs* and *She Is Asleep*. Cage's Asian interests were reflected via a complete
performance of the *Sonatas and Interludes*, and his moves toward indeterminacy
and tape composition by *Music for Carillon No. 1* and *Williams Mix*. The climax
of the concert came with the first performance of the major new work that had
occupied Cage for the previous several months, the *Concert for Piano and Orchestra*
(1957–58), which is dedicated to Elaine de Kooning. The choice of *concert* rather
than *concerto* in the title is an indication that each of the performers is a soloist.
Apart from the central *Solo for Piano*—which can be performed separately—there
are parts for three violins, two violas, cello, double bass, flute (doubling alto flute
and piccolo), clarinet, bassoon (doubling saxophone), trumpet, trombone, and
tuba; some, all, or none of these may be included in a performance of the work.

John Cage and Merce Cunningham, London, 1964. Photograph by Hans Wild. Used by permission of the John Cage Trust.

Finally, there is also a separate part for the conductor—Merce Cunningham at the Town Hall premiere—who indicates the passing of time (and thus acts as a human chronometric cueing device for the performers) by making slow, circular, clockwise sweeping gestures with his or her arms.

The thirteen instrumental parts were composed in a manner similar to the point-drawing system of the *Music for Piano* series. However, in this case, different sizes of note-head were used to indicate dynamics and/or duration, while chance operations determined which sounds, from a precompositional set devised for each instrument, were to be notated. Much more complex is the highly virtuosic *Solo for Piano*, written specifically for David Tudor. It consists of sixty-three individual pages, which between them contain eighty-four different types of notation. As determined by *I Ching*–derived chance operations (and in a manner partly analogous to the creation of the text of "45' for a Speaker"), some of the notations are derived from wholly new compositional processes, while others are either repetitions of, or variations on, such processes. The placement of the notations, as well as the rectangular spaces they occupy, were also determined randomly. Overall, this leads in visual terms to fragments of music—none of them written in conventional format—being juxtaposed on each page and, in some cases, to notations spilling across pages.

Tudor's involvement in the project—as in so many others—was crucial, as Cage was able to capitalize on his considerable creative and re-creative talents in posing major challenges to the performer of the *Solo for Piano*. First, Tudor had painstakingly to devise appropriate strategies for the interpretation of the notations, whether premeditated or spontaneous, precise or vague; subsequently, those interpretational strategies had to be translated equally painstakingly into physical performance actions. Finally, and perhaps most importantly, came the decisions as to which notations should actually be performed, and in what order: Cage allowed Tudor (and later performers) complete freedom of choice in this fundamental aspect of the work's character, one consequence of which is the potential for widely differing durations for separate renditions of the piece.[26]

One by-product of the Twenty-Five-Year Retrospective Concert was the (re)birth of Cage's career as a visual artist. Although his major work in this field only began in 1978, he had previously experimented with painting in the 1930s. In 1958, in conjunction with the Town Hall concert, manuscript pages from the *Concert for Piano and Orchestra*, together with *Water Music* and *Haiku* (1958), were exhibited upstairs at the Stable Gallery as works of art in their own right; a number were sold, and the exhibition as a whole (which was paired with a Rauschenberg exhibition in the main downstairs gallery) received favorable comment in the press. Indeed, one aspect of Cage's work from this period—its calligraphic precision and visual beauty—became increasingly important as he moved away from determinate notation. An example of this tendency is the score of *Water Music* (see page 57), but there are numerous others. And even in those works that appear relatively conventional in their notation, Cage appears to be increasingly aware of their visual impact. Thus the piece that almost immediately preceded the *Concert*—*Winter Music* (1957) for one to twenty pianists—is exquisitely laid out and yet challenging to its performer(s). Each of the score's twenty pages contains between one and sixty-one chords, scattered over its surface, and consisting of either a cluster or—more usually—one to ten pitches. These are placed, quasi-conventionally, on standard five-line staves; but indeterminacy is effected through the ambiguity of the clefs used and the numbers of pitches assigned (by the performers) to each clef.[27] Further indeterminacies result from two considerations:

John Cage, David Tudor, and Sandra Neels, playing an electrified piano, Les Baux, France, 1964. *Photographer unknown. Used by permission of the John Cage Trust.*

first, the order of notations on each page is free; and second, in any performance, some or all of the twenty pages may be used in any order and/or superimposed. Thus, from a finite set of materials, an infinite number of different performances may result. In David Tudor's case, the creation of a performing version of the score involved a huge amount of preparatory work.[28]

Following the *succès de scandale* of the Twenty-Five-Year Retrospective Concert—which Virgil Thomson, in a later review of its recording on Avakian, described as "'a jolly good row and a good show'"[29]—Cage and Tudor again spent the late summer and fall of 1958 in Europe, visiting Darmstadt, Stockholm, Brussels, Cologne, and Milan. Darmstadt, in particular—where Cage taught at the Fereinkurse [vacation course] für Neue Musik—proved to be something of a turning point in his career. Boulez had originally been slated as the featured composer but pulled out; at the suggestion of Bruno Maderna, Cage was (at short notice) invited to substitute for him.[30] Among the novelties sprung on Darmstadt's unsuspecting audience were the first performance of *Variations I* (1958) and the series of lectures collectively titled "Composition as Process."[31] Already upset by his 1954 reception at Donaueschingen, and presumably incensed by Boulez's 1957 article "Aléa" (in which his former friend appropriated certain aspects of Cage's chance processes while simultaneously condemning Cage's own uses of them), Cage deliberately—in Christopher Shultis's words—threw down the gauntlet to his European contemporaries.[32]

In his first lecture, "Changes," Cage described the "changes that have taken place in my compositional means, with particular reference to what, a decade ago, I termed 'structure' and 'method.'"[33] Printed in four vertical columns per page, "Changes" has the same overall length as the *Music of Changes*; the "silent" gaps in the text were intended to be filled by the corresponding fragments of the piano piece. The second lecture, "Indeterminacy," has no musical component but rather discusses in considerable detail a number of compositions that are indeterminate with respect to their performance. The examples cited by Cage range from Bach's *Art of Fugue* to pieces by Brown, Feldman, and Wolff; but the lecture goes out of its way to criticize the recently composed *Klavierstück XI* by Karlheinz Stockhausen (born 1928), one of Boulez's principal associates at the time. Finally, in "Communication," Cage launched a multiple attack on Boulez ("If one of us says that all twelve tones should be in a row and another says they shouldn't, which one of us is right?"); on what he saw as the European fixation with answers rather than questions; and on his immediate audience at Darmstadt ("Why is it so difficult for so many people to listen? . . . Are they stupid?").[34]

Inevitably, the public reaction to Cage's Darmstadt visit was very negative, and he did not attend the festival again until 1990. But it is clear that Cage intended to provoke such a reaction, for he seems by this point to have decided unequivocally to reposition himself in relation to the contemporary music scene. Prior to the mid-1950s, he had seemingly considered himself part of an international, Euro-American radical movement: in his writings and elsewhere, he had emphasized his studies with Schoenberg, enthused about Satie and Webern, and temporarily aligned himself with Boulez. But now, increasingly treated as an outsider—and in some cases ridiculed—by the European avant-garde, Cage came to view himself as a purely American composer, coming from a New World tradition that, to a considerable degree, had distanced itself from the concerns of the Old World. Thus, in response to a request from Darmstadt's Wolfgang Steinecke for an article for the *Darmstädter Beitrage*, Cage wrote his "History of Experimental Music in the United States" (1959).[35]

In this text, which Christopher Shultis has rightly characterized as a "'declaration of independence' from European influence,"[36] Cage argues that it is no longer necessary to be concerned with "tonality or atonality, Schoenberg or Stravinsky . . . nor with consonance or dissonance."[37] Instead, he privileges "noises [that] are as useful to new music as so-called musical tones" and champions such figures as his teacher (Cowell) and Varèse.[38] He also praises Wolff and Feldman, as well as several of his American experimentalist predecessors and contemporaries, at the expense of such quasi-European composers as Carl Ruggles and Elliott Carter. And while he still notes the "vitality that characterizes the current European musical scene [that] follows from the activities of Boulez, Stockhausen, Nono, Maderna, Pousseur, Berio, etc.," he sees "in all of this activity an element of tradition, continuity with the past."[39] Or, as he puts it more pointedly elsewhere, "It must be very difficult for you in Europe to write music, for you are so close to the centers of tradition."[40]

There is one other aspect of the musical relationship between Europe and America that Cage alludes to in "History of Experimental Music in the United States": the degree to which the tide of influence had turned in America's favor. Cage merely notes that "[t]he silences of American experimental music and even its technical involvements with chance operations are being introduced into new European music."[41] But thirty years later, his friend Morton Feldman was rather more direct: "'I find Earle [Brown] was a kind of bridge between Europe and America. And I think that as a tangible influence, Brown, by his notation and by his plastic forms, has influenced Europe more than the rest of us. . . . I think he's been ripped off more than any of us, in an overt way. The rip-off of Cage is, to some degree, disguised. And the rip-off of myself to some degree gets into the world of a philosophical approach that might influence somebody, rather than the music itself.'"[42] Specific examples of the kind of appropriations Feldman mentions are not difficult to identify: in his article, he points to the notation of *Circles* (1960) by Luciano Berio (1925–2003) and the loops of Witold Lutosławski (1913–94) as being directly influenced by Brown. Brown's first visits to Europe were in 1956 and 1958, and three of his works from this period—*Pentathis* (1957), *Available Forms 1* (1961), and *Available Forms 2* (1962)—were premiered there. The variable structures of the latter two pieces set a clear precedent for Stockhausen's *Momente* (1961–69). There are countless other examples of American innovations being appropriated by their European colleagues: focusing solely on Stockhausen's work, there are obvious borrowings in his *Klavierstück VI* (1955) from Cage's *Music of Changes* and *31' 57.9864"*; in *Klavierstück XI* (1956) from Feldman's *Intermission 6* (1953); in the use of a movable plastic transparency in *Refrain* (1959) from Cage's *Variations I* and *Fontana Mix* (both 1958); and in the use of star charts in his *Sternklang* (1971) from Cage's *Atlas Eclipticalis* (1961).[43]

After leaving Darmstadt, Cage and Tudor traveled to Stockholm and subsequently Brussels, where, at the World's Fair in October 1958, they gave a two-piano recital. A further concert featured *Variations I* and the premiere of *Music Walk* (1958), though a proposed dance by Merce Cunningham and Carolyn Brown (to a piano reduction of Earle Brown's *Indices*) had to be canceled due to the death of Pope Pius XII. The final Brussels engagement saw Cage deliver a new text piece, originally titled "Indeterminacy: New Aspect of Form in Instrumental and Electronic Music." Developed from an idea of David Tudor's, it consisted of thirty stories, each lasting one minute. The next year, in preparation for a further rendition in the United States, Cage added another sixty stories, and it was this ninety-minute version that was recorded by Folkways, with accompaniment by Tudor. Cage continued to add stories, and substantial selections appear in *Silence* and *A Year from Monday*. In *Silence*, the largest grouping is a block of fifty-eight appearing under the title "Indeterminacy"; in the latter, a further block of thirty-five stories appears as "How to Pass, Kick, Fall, and Run."[44] This was the title of a 1965 Cunningham dance, Cage's accompaniment to which consisted of him reading eighteen or nineteen of the one-minute stories. Most of these stories—which have contributed in no small part to the Cagean mythology—are concerned with "things that happened and stuck in my mind" and as such are at least partially autobiographical. Others "I read in books and remembered," while "still others have been told to me by friends."[45] However, given that each story, regardless of its length, was designed to be performed in one minute and that the intended effect of the set was undoubtedly to be "a wholly delightful distillation of Cage's irrepressible humor, his high spirits, and his surprising clarity of expression,"[46] there is always the suspicion that complete factual accuracy may at times have been subservient to memorability. Be that as it may, "Indeterminacy," in its recorded form, certainly struck a chord—albeit a dissonant one—with Cage's mother. (His parents were by this time living in New Jersey.) As reported in the post-recording version of the lecture printed in *Silence*, Crete's reaction was typically introspective and critical: "I've listened to your record several times. After hearing all those stories about your childhood, I keep asking myself, 'Where was it that I failed?'"[47]

After a visit to Cologne, Cage spent November 1958 through March 1959 in Milan; there, at the invitation of Berio, he worked at the electronic music studio of Radio Audizione Italienne. Cage's first compositional act after his arrival was the creation of what James Pritchett has aptly termed a "musical tool."[48] Like *Variations I*, this tool—ultimately named *Fontana Mix* after Cage's Milanese landlady, Signora Fontana—consists not of a "conventional" score notated on paper but rather of a set of marked transparencies. In terms of their graphic constituents, *Variations I* and *Fontana Mix* are derived from fixed notations that had first appeared in the *Solo for Piano;* but now the constituent elements became mobile in relation to each other.[49] In general terms, both works consist of a series of transparencies marked with lines, dots, or grids. Through the superimpositions of these materials, and in accordance with the variable parameters defined by Cage's instructions, the performer makes measurements to determine such matters as the types of sound to be used as well as their durations, dynamics, and so on. The role of the performer in creating the final (performed) work is thus extended and developed significantly. A number of other pieces from this period—including *Music Walk* (1958), *Music for Amplified Toy Pianos* (1960), *WBAI* (1960), *Music for "The Marrying Maiden"* (1960), *Cartridge Music* (1960), *Solo for Voice 2* (1960), and especially *Variations II* (1961)—make similar use of transparencies, sometimes in conjunction with notations fixed on paper. In addition, some of these "tool" pieces were used to generate further works: the *Fontana Mix* materials were employed in the creation of a tape piece—also (and somewhat confusingly) called *Fontana Mix*—as well as the virtuosic *Aria* (1958) for solo voice, *Sounds of Venice* and *Water Walk* (both 1959; both for solo performer), and *Theatre Piece* (1960) for one to eight performers. In the case of *Cartridge Music*, the original intention had been to create new sounds (usually too quiet to be heard) via the "insertion, use, and removal of objects from the [phonograph] cartridge, manipulation of timbre and amplitude dials of the associated amplifiers, [and the] production of auxiliary sounds."[50] But the score materials were also employed in the writing of several lectures, including the quadrilogue "Where Are We Going? and What Are We Doing?" (1960).[51] *WBAI* became a "mixing tool" during the period of Cage's Norton Lectures in 1988–89. One other point worth noting here is the degree to which Cage's work of this period engaged with theater. This feature was already explicit in *Water Music;* it was further extended in *Aria, Music Walk, Sounds of Venice, Water Walk*, and—most obviously—*Theatre Piece*. Theatricality is also an important element in many of Cage's lectures from the 1950s onwards, as should be clear from the discussions of those texts elsewhere in this book, as well as in such later pieces as *o' oo"* (1962), *Variations IV* (1963), *Variations V* (1965), *Variations VII* (1966), *Reunion* (1968), *HPSCHD* (1967–69), *Song Books* (1970), and so on.

Apart from his compositional activities at the radio station, Cage's time in Milan was important for another reason: he became a television celebrity, as a result of his appearances on the popular quiz show "Lascia o Raddoppia" (which might very loosely be translated as "Double Your Money").[52] Over the course of five weeks, Cage answered progressively more difficult questions on mushrooms; and each week he prefaced the quiz element of his appearance with a short musical performance. In week one he played the prepared-piano solos from *Amores*, and in later weeks performed such new works as *Water Walk* and *Sounds of Venice*. Following his success in the fifth and final week—answering questions on the genera of white-spored mushrooms—Cage collected his prize of five million lire (roughly eight thousand dollars in 1959). Upon returning to America, he spent his winnings on a new Steinway grand (its predecessor having been a casualty of the move to Stony Point) and a Volkswagen microbus that he presented to the Cunningham Dance Company.

New Audiences

If the calendar year 1952 had been Cage's musical *annus mirabilis*, then the academic year 1960–61 ran it a close second in more general terms, as several events conspired to bring him to a wide, and mainly international, audience. First, he found a publisher for his music. By this point, Cage had completed around 120 works; yet, amazingly, only one—*Amores*—had been made commercially available, through its 1943 publication in Cowell's *New Music*. In the early 1950s, through Stockhausen, there had been some correspondence with Universal Edition, but this, like the later discussions Cage held with Schirmers, had come to nothing. Requests for Cage's scores were increasing each year and as a consequence were taking up more and more of his precious time. Finally, in the midst of work on the tape composition for Jackson MacLow's play *The Marrying Maiden*, Cage decided to write nothing further until he had found a publisher. What subsequently transpired, in Cage's 1980 version of the story, has the same ring of unlikely serendipity as his initial contact with Richard Buhlig back in 1933. "I picked up the Yellow Pages and I ran down the list of music publishers, and I stopped at Peters. The reason I stopped there was because someone—I think someone in some string quartet—had said that Mr. Hinrichsen [Walter Hinrichsen, who had established C. F. Peters's New York office in 1948] was interested in American music. So I simply called and asked to speak with him. He said, very cheerfully over the phone, 'I'm so glad that you called. My wife [Evelyn Hinrichsen] has always wanted me to publish your music.' That day we had lunch and signed the contract."[53]

The second important event of 1960–61 was Cage's appointment as a fellow at the Center for Advanced Studies at Wesleyan University in Connecticut. Cage's connections with Wesleyan went back to the mid-1950s, when Richard K. Winslow—a member of the university's music faculty—had engaged Cage and Tudor to give a concert. Winslow twice invited them back and was also instrumental in nominating Cage to the fellowship.[54] During his time at Wesleyan, Cage engaged with the student body in various ways; wrote the "Lecture on Commitment" and "Rhythm Etc.";[55] met the faculty member Norman O. Brown, who became a friend and a champion of Cage; and, over a nine-month period, completed a major new orchestral work. *Atlas Eclipticalis* (1961) was commissioned by the Montreal Festival Society and first performed—simultaneously with *Winter Music*—at the International Week of Today's Music in Montreal in August 1961. The basic compositional process used in *Atlas Eclipticalis* is similar in many respects to the earlier point-drawing systems; here, however, the "points" were generated by a set of large star charts that Cage discovered at the Wesleyan observatory. Chance operations and transparencies were used to create random tracings of star locations, which were then transferred to the paper instrumental parts. In the star charts, relative brightness was indicated by relative size; in the instrumental parts of *Atlas Eclipticalis*, relative size translates into relative amplitude. Provision is made for eighty-six instruments. Some or all may be used in any given performance, and some or all may be electronically amplified. Each of the instrumental parts is dedicated to a relative, friend, or associate of Cage. The general instructions that apply to the interpretation of the parts—typed onto a single sheet—are succinct and direct, not least in their description of the conductor who, in a manner similar to that found in the *Concert*, "performs a circle like that of a watch-hand. . . . The conductor's time will be at least twice as slow as clock time."

The Montreal premiere, conducted by Cage, seems to have passed without incident. But a later series of performances, given in 1964 by the New York Philharmonic Orchestra (conducted not by Leonard Bernstein but by a mechanical device made by Paul Williams) achieved notoriety as a result of the behavior of the orchestral players. The work had been programmed, along with pieces by Brown and Feldman, as part of a major avant-garde series. Although Bernstein acted seriously and responsibly in the main—as did the orchestra during the rehearsal period—his initial response to the use of contact microphones was rather unhelpful.[56] However, after the second of the week's performances, the orchestra hissed Cage; during the third, they talked and laughed, played scales and melodies rather than the notated material, sang or whistled into their contact microphones, and in some cases deliberately destroyed the electronic equipment. After a serious rebuke from Bernstein and the union representative, the final performance passed without incident, but the experience left Cage furious: sixteen years later, he could still speak of the musicians' behavior in (for him) uniquely savage terms:

> The New York Philharmonic is a bad orchestra. They're like a group of gangsters. They have no shame—when I came off stage after one of those performances, one of them who had played badly shook my hand, smiled, and said, "Come back in ten years; we'll treat you better." They turn things away from music, and from any professional attitude toward music, to some kind of a social situation that is not very beautiful.
>
> In the case of *Atlas* they destroyed my property. They acted criminally. They tore the microphones off the instruments and stamped on them, and the next day I had to buy new ones to replace them for the next performance. It was very costly. And they weren't ashamed.[57]

At the root of Cage's anger was the fact that the Philharmonic players had abnegated their responsibilities in failing to employ a quality he believed was fundamental to the proper performance of his music: discipline.

The final—and in some ways most important—event of 1960–61 was the publication of *Silence*. Richard K. Winslow was again instrumental in this, as "he inspired the [Wesleyan] University Press to publish [the] book."[58] This first collection of Cage's writings brought him to a far wider audience than would otherwise have been possible. But, as David Patterson has noted, the effect of such exposure was not wholly positive: "While considered a 'classic' text in Cage studies, *Silence* also documents the ways in which such collections have skewed conceptions of Cage both biographically and aesthetically. . . . Owing to the deliberately nonchronological ordering of [its contents]—an ordering that Cage himself determined in this case—the inattentive reader can easily confuse Cage's writings of one period with those of another."[59] In addition, the book contains some important factual inaccuracies—such as its dating of "The Future of Music: Credo" to 1937—that have led to further misunderstandings and misinterpretations. That said, given its concatenation of almost all of Cage's important writings prior to 1960—the only major exceptions being the "Juilliard Lecture" and "A Composer's Confessions"—*Silence* played a vital role in introducing Cage's radical ideas to the open-minded generation of the 1960s. As Wilfrid Mellers noted on the jacket of the first British imprint, "*Silence* is a bible for the young in heart."

Towards Infinity

There were two longer-term results of the various developments of 1960–61. First, if there was a specific point at which Cage became "Cage"—to invoke the title of Thomas Hines's 1994 study of the composer's early years—it was probably around this time. Before 1960, Cage had slowly but surely accumulated a certain amount of notoriety (if not fame) in America and parts of Europe. But with the signing of the exclusive contract with C. F. Peters, and especially the publication of *Silence*, Cage ceased solely to be a person and instead began a new life as a personality. More significantly still, the man came increasingly to be replaced by a myth, partly of the man's own making. This is particularly noticeable in the large number of (often autobiographical) stories that adorn the pages of *Silence*, whether in the collected form of "Indeterminacy"[60] or the more haphazard arrangement that maintains elsewhere. From the 1960s on, as Cage's celebrity grew, through the many interviews he gave and the numerous anecdotal remarks he made in his interviews and his writings, the creation of a Cagean myth—and the invention of "Cage"—was inevitable. Cage was hardly unique among artists in painting a self-portrait that emphasized his best features—Charles Ives is similar in this respect—but, as was suggested at the outset of this book, it has become an increasing priority for scholars, since Cage's death, to "clean up" the portrait he left us by searching anew for the person behind the personality and for the man behind the myth.

The second, and less positive, effect of Cage's newfound fame (though not necessarily fortune) was that even greater demands were now placed on his time. This is one plausible reason that has been given to explain the surprising contraction in his compositional activities during the remainder of the 1960s. As James Pritchett has pointed out, "In the eight-year period of 1952 to 1959 . . . [Cage] completed about forty compositions. . . . In the eight-year period of 1962 to 1969, on the other hand, Cage completed only about fifteen pieces."[61] Given his new arrangement with C. F. Peters, this was all the more ironic. A related factor, also discussed by Pritchett, was Cage's "discomfort with all the attention that was being paid to him," which "got in the way of his deeply-felt need to pursue the new and original."[62] One solution to these problems was a partial reversal of his aesthetic: whereas previously "he had attempted to make his musical works be more like life, he now turned to transforming his life into his work."[63] Such a reading certainly explains Cage's tendency, in pieces like *o' oo"* (1962) and *Rozart Mix* (1965), to follow a quasi-Duchampian path in allowing music to become "whatever it was that Cage was doing." And there is a parallel to this in the increasingly "personal, chatty, anecdotal, and aphoristic" nature of his writings during this period.[64] In addition, it is significant that in the foreword to *A Year from Monday* (1967), Cage states quite openly that he had become "less and less interested in music."[65]

However, if one views Cage's activities of the 1960s in toto, it becomes clear that there was actually no lessening of his activity: rather, that activity became diversified. Apart from his compositions, Cage also produced the bulk of his substantial "Diary: How to Improve the World (You Will Only Make Matters Worse)," parts of which appeared in *A Year from Monday* and *M: Writings '67–'72*.[66] The time required by the daily, chance-ordered routine of compiling this diary should not be underestimated; nor, more importantly, should the depth and breadth of thought that underpins it be disregarded, for Cage shows here his intellectual brilliance and virtuosity in bringing together a huge diversity of ideas—notably those of Marshall McLuhan and R. Buckminster Fuller—into a compelling, albeit mosaic, whole. And while the tone of the writing is indeed "personal, chatty, anecdotal, and aphoristic," the "Diary" is also, like the lectures from the early 1950s, "both an explanation and a concrete demonstration of ideas."[67] In the header to the first installment of 1965, Cage described his modus operandi: "For each day, I determined by chance operations how many parts of the mosaic I would write and how many words there would be in each. The number of words per day was to equal, or, by the last statement written, to exceed one hundred words. . . . I used an IBM Selectric typewriter to print my text. I used twelve different type faces, letting chance operations determine which face would be used for each statement. So, too, the left marginations were determined, the right marginations being the result of not hyphenating words and at the same time keeping the number of characters per line forty-three or less."[68] While it is not practical to reproduce here the original typography, the following excerpt from the first installment gives some sense of the layout and the topical density of the "Diary":

III. AS McLUHAN SAYS,
EVERYTHING HAPPENS AT ONCE. IMAGE IS
NO LONGER STREAM FALLING OVER ROCKS,
GETTING FROM ORIGINAL TO FINAL PLACE;
IT'S AS TENNEY EXPLAINED: A VIBRATING
COMPLEX, ANY ADDITION OR SUBTRACTION
OF COMPONENT(S), REGARDLESS OF APPARENT
POSITION(S) IN THE TOTAL SYSTEM,
PRODUCING ALTERATION, A DIFFERENT MUSIC.
FULLER: AS LONG AS ONE HUMAN BEING IS
HUNGRY, THE ENTIRE HUMAN RACE IS
HUNGRY. City planning's obsolete. What's
needed is global planning so Earth
may stop stepping like octopus on its
own feet. Buckminster Fuller uses his
head: comprehensive design science;
inventory of world resources. Conversion:
the mind turns around, no longer
facing in its direction. Utopia?
Self-knowledge. Some will make it,
with or without LSD. The others? Pray
for acts of God, crises, power
failures, no water to drink.[69]

Another area of expanding activity related to Cage's responsibilities as musical director of the Cunningham Dance Company. Just as Cage's career had taken off after 1961, so had Cunningham's, to the point where in 1964 the company (including Cage) spent six months engaged in a world tour that took them from western Europe, through Czechoslovakia and Poland, to India, Thailand, and Japan.[70] And whereas in the 1940s and 1950s Cage's collaborations with Cunningham had centered mainly on short works for small forces, by the mid-1960s the norm was more of such major projects as the audiovisual, multicollaboratorial extravaganza *Variations V* (1965), once described by Gordon Mumma as "the first Wagnerian thing [Cage] did."[71] The work was presented at least seventeen times in America and Canada, as well as in Europe.[72] Similarly "Wagnerian" in scope (though not involving dancers) were *Variations VII* (1966), *Musicircus* (1967), *Reunion* (1968), *33 1/3* (1969), and *HPSCHD* (1967–69, co-composed with Lejaren Hiller[1924–94]), this last requiring "7 harpsichordists, 208 tapes, 84 slide projectors, 52 tape recorders, 52 speakers, 12 movie projectors, a 340–foot circular

John Cage with David Tudor and Gordon Mumma (foreground), providing music for a performance of Variations V *(1965), music by John Cage, film by Stan VanDerBeek, and TV images by Nam June Paik, 1965. On stage are Carolyn Brown, Merce Cunningham, and Barbara Dilley. Photograph by Herve Gloaguen. Used by permission of the John Cage Trust.*

plastic screen, as well as amplifiers, additional plastic screens, slides, films, posters, and other materials."[73]

A brief description of *HPSCHD* will give some indication of the time-consuming complexities its composition and realization involved. Although it originated in a commission from the Swiss harpsichordist Antoinette Vischer—who performed one of the seven solos at the premiere—the basic idea in *HPSCHD* (which is the computer abbreviation for "harpsichord") was "'to explore microtonality. Thus, the many scales, equal divisions of the octave, and so forth.'"[74] Cage's co-composer, Lejaren Hiller, was a computer specialist; he and Cage together devised a number of computer programs. The first—DICEGAME—generated the material for the seven harpsichord solos, using principles derived from Mozart's *Musi-kalisches Würfelspiel* (Musical dice game; ка294d). Of these, Solo II is a realization of the original dice game; Solos III and IV also use the dice game, but with other Mozart pieces substituted for the dice-game measures; Solos V and VI are similar but with the substitute material now chosen from the post-Mozartian keyboard literature; Solo VII allows its performer "to play any Mozart composition or any piece the other soloists happen to be playing," while Solo I is "a transcription of one of the tape-orchestra parts for the twelve-tone gamut."[75]

The tape-orchestra parts were generated by a second computer program—HPSCHD—which produced material in divisions of the octave from five to fifty-six. In performance, the 208 tapes that resulted were played on fifty-two tape recorders, over fifty-two separate loudspeakers. However, given that "the pitch materials delved into the world of microcollage," it was decided that the visual aspects of the work would "fittingly [explore] the world of macrocollage."[76] Accordingly, Calvin Sumsion and Ronald Nameth assembled, respectively, approximately 1,600 hand-painted slides—featuring everything from computer printouts to an armadillo—and a selection of films that showed "mankind's conception and experience of space subjectively and intuitively"[77] and the more objective viewpoint obtained from scientific films of outer space. The various visual images were projected onto "eleven parallel screens made of transparent plastic" and a "gigantic circular veil (also of translucent plastic) 340 feet in circumference."[78] The first performance of *HPSCHD* took place in the Assembly Hall of the University of Illinois at Urbana-Champaign; it lasted four hours and was attended by almost seven thousand people.

Several features of *HPSCHD*—and by extension of Cage's other "Wagnerian" works of the late 1960s—should be highlighted here. First, the amount of precompositional and preperformance work each piece required was huge, not least as a result of their reliance on technology. Second, the number of Cage's collaborators in these pieces—and the nature of the various collaborations—effectively resulted for the first time in Cage fully achieving his long-stated ambition of "finding ways of composing that would free the music, free the sound from my memory and my likes and dislikes."[79] And third, for the freely mobile spectators at events such as *Musicircus* and *HPSCHD*, the whole nature of "audience" changed: as Cage had put it in his 1955 article "Experimental Music: Doctrine," "[E]ach human being is at the best point for reception," the implication being that the focus of any given work should not be the score or its performance but rather its reception by individual auditors. Or, to put it another way, "Composing's one thing, performing's another, listening's a third. What can they have to do with one another?"[80]

HPSCHD was one result of Cage's two-year residency at the University of Illinois at Urbana-Champaign (1967–69), and the decade also saw him accepting appointments at the University of Cincinnati (1967) and the University of California at Davis (1969). His involvement in media other than music was further demonstrated in his coordination of the book *Notations* (1969) and in the creation of the 1969 plexigram project *Not Wanting to Say Anything about Marcel*, an *in memoriam* to Duchamp, with whom he had become very close.[81] A final demand on Cage's time in the 1960s resulted from his family responsibilities. By the start of the decade his father was seventy-four and his mother seventy-five; as an only child, John Jr. was their main source of financial and emotional support, and this was a duty he took very seriously. John Sr. died in 1964, and Crete in 1969; and as anyone who has lost a parent will know, the days spent in dealing with such practical matters as funerals and wills are insignificantly few in comparison to the weeks and months required by the process of grieving.

There is, however, another explanation that might be posited in relation to Cage's compositional "inactivity" of the 1960s, one that results from the fundamental nature of the work he was producing. In 1952, with *4' 33"*, Cage had liberated ambient sound. A decade later, with *0' 00"* (whose subtitle is *4' 33" No. 2*), Cage achieved the same degree of liberation for everyday gesture: a typical performance was that given in May 1965 at Brandeis University's Rose Art Museum, when all of Cage's actions—"sitting on a squeaky chair . . . writing letters on a typewriter, and occasionally drinking from a glass of water"—were massively amplified.[82] But with *Variations IV* (1963), Cage in a sense liberated *everything*: the materials that constitute the work's score do not enable the performers to specify substance (i.e., sonic material) but rather the means by which the spatial *sources* of such substance may be determined. In other words, the performers are not told what sounds to make but how to determine where the sounds should come from. The work is designated as being "for any number of players, any sounds or combinations of sounds produced by any means, with or without other activities," and can be performed anywhere—concert hall, theater, apartment, open space, or cave. In Cage's own recorded performance of the work's premiere, at the Fiegen/Palmer Gallery in Los Angeles, there is extensive use not only of amplified ambient sounds (of street, audience, and radio) but also of discs of a wide variety of extant musics. However, this does not justify Eric Salzman's jocular description of the work as the "'kitchen-sink sonata, the everything piece, the minestrone masterpiece of modern music.'" Rather, it necessitates a reading of *Variations IV* as a McLuhanesque example of "instant communication with the entire experiential world, [in which] our nervous systems are extended [and receive] messages from every corner of the global village."[83] In *Variations IV,* Cage opens out an infinite performative universe, which can contain everything that has existed previously and predict everything that is yet to come. In this context, it is hardly surprising that for the remaining years of the decade he found it difficult to produce anything, at least in music, that was genuinely new. Rather, the remaining *Variations* pieces, *Musicircus, 33 ⅓,* and even *HPSCHD* can seem simply to be regurgitations of *Variations IV.* Ten years earlier, following his composition of *December 1952,* Earle Brown had found himself wondering what else, musically, there was that he could achieve: "'The extremely high degree of . . . freedom . . . seemed to be as far as I could go in that direction.'"[84] Following the composition of *Variations IV,* Cage must have understood Brown's feelings exactly.

4 | New York #2,
1970–92

CAGE'S REASONS FOR MOVING to Stony Point in 1954 had been partly practical—necessitated by the demolition of Bozza Mansion—but also, one suspects, partly ideological: he must have been intrigued by the possibility of becoming a member of an idealistic artistic community and was certainly tempted by the prospect of developing a Center for Experimental Music. Furthermore, he became increasingly interested in anarchy during the 1960s—as he puts it in its simplest terms in the foreword to *A Year from Monday*, "I'd like our activities to be more social and anarchically so"[1]—and the unconventional nature of the Stony Point arrangements must also have appealed to him. During Cage's time at Stony Point, some things certainly improved: for instance, his initial accommodations in the wasp-infested farmhouse attic were exchanged for the more comfortable two-room cabin described by Ninette Lyon. But, once again, the intended Center for Experimental Music failed to materialize. Cage had, during the 1960s, spent increasing amounts of time away from Stony Point, and by 1970 the original dream had been shattered. As he describes it in *For the Birds*, by this time the community had become "like a shanty town: the roads are no longer maintained, the garbage is no longer collected. . . . And then, I am getting older; in the winter I'm afraid of the ice."[2] There were also ideological concerns: "[A]las, the truth is that I'm becoming an absentee landlord, exactly what disgusted Thoreau. I have become an owner who doesn't use what he possesses. In our age, that's a transgression of morality. I have become immoral."[3] Cage's solution to this problem was to move back to Manhattan. In September 1970 he became cohabiter of Cunningham's basement apartment in the West Village. Subsequently, the couple moved to a loft on Bank Street and eventually, in 1978, to an apartment in the former B. Altman department store, at the intersection of Sixth Avenue and West Eighteenth Street.[4]

A more speculative—quasi-Freudian—view might also be taken, though, of Cage's moves from and to New York City and of the revitalization of his compositional activities that followed his return to urban life in 1970. Since at least 1952, Cage's parents had been based on the East Coast, initially in Manhattan and then from 1954 in Upper Montclair, New Jersey. Just as, in 1938, Cage's departure from Los Angeles might be interpreted as an attempt to escape from his parents' potentially stifling influence, the move to Stony Point might be seen as having been designed literally to put some distance between himself and them. Even this

John Cage, working at his Eighteenth Street loft in New York, with Losa, September 1991. *Photograph by Rene Block. Used by permission of the John Cage Trust.*

physical separation, though, could not curtail Crete's penchant for criticizing her son's work. In 1954, after a performance of the *Music of Changes*, Crete had said to Earle Brown, "'[D]on't you think that John has gone too far this time?'"[5] Her reaction to the recording of "Indeterminacy" has already been cited; and when, in 1967 in the context of the "Diary: How to Improve the World (You Will Only Make Matters Worse)," the fifty-five-year-old Cage informed his mother that he was writing about world improvement, she exclaimed, "'John! How *dare* you? You should be ashamed! I'm surprised at you.'"[6]

Cage's relationship with his parents includes some interestingly anomalous features that, once again, suggest comparisons with the experiences of Charles Ives. First, while many of Cage's stories and anecdotes concerning his father are couched in warm and affectionate language—and often express pride in John Sr.'s achievements—the majority of those concerning his mother tend to focus on her frequently harsh criticisms. Second, although a number of photographs survive of John Sr., either alone or with John Jr., only one photograph of Crete appears to be extant (reproduced on page 8, dating from the mid-1920s). Third, Cage almost invariably referred to John Sr. using the familiar and familial "Dad," but his other parent is usually characterized via the formal "Mother" or the even-more-distant "Crete." See, for instance, Cage's comments in an interview with Stephen Montague, or the titles of two unpublished piano pieces dating from 1945, *Dad* and *Crete*.[7]

Whatever his relationship with his parents, however, by 1970 John Sr. and Crete had passed away, and Cage no longer needed to be based a seventy-five-minute drive away from them. Just as one door—connecting Cage to his biographical past (as the necessarily prospective son of an inventor)—had been closed, so perhaps in reaction it now became possible for him to open another door to a new creative period based much more than had previously been feasible in musical retrospection.

New Beginnings

One consequence of Cage's composition of *Variations IV* was that the musical universe became infinitely expanded; indeed, there can be no boundaries—and therefore no forefront—in a universe as limitless as that predicated by the work. As Feldman put it in 1985, Cage had "stepped aside to such a degree that we see the end of the world, the end of art."[8] Thus the conventional view of radicalism—based solely on prospective expansion, and roughly analogous to cosmology's Big Bang theory—failed sufficiently to explain the realities of the contemporary musical situation in which Cage found himself. A more plausible explanation—which could take into account the effects not only of prospection (Cage's "deeply-felt need to pursue the new and original") but also of the retrospection and extraspection made possible by technological advance—lay rather in an analogy with cosmology's steady-state hypothesis, where "new" material is created not intrinsically but rather through the infinite hybridic recombinations and reworkings of existing material. Music had previously moved forward; after *Variations IV* it could only go round and round.

Whether this interpretation was consciously, or even subconsciously, recognized by Cage is moot; one suspects it was not. But from 1970 onwards it seems clear that one way in which he realized his work could continue was through its reinterpretation of existing musical—and other—objects. Cage had made reference to the past in some of his earlier work: examples include the LP recordings that appear almost as *objets trouvés* in *Credo in Us* (1942), *Imaginary Landscape No. 5* (1952), and Cage's own performance of *Variations IV*; and there are "live" citations of existing music or musical styles in *Credo in Us*, as well as Cage's two homages to Mozart—*A Book of Music* (1944) and *HPSCHD* (1967–69). But starting with *Cheap Imitation* (1969), this previously sporadic tendency becomes much more consistent in Cage's music and his writings. That said, the particular factors that led him to the composition of *Cheap Imitation* were highly unusual and completely unplanned.

Although Cage's enthusiasm for the music of Webern had long since waned—primarily, it might be surmised, as a result of his encounters with Boulez and others of Webern's self-appointed heirs—his love of Erik Satie had grown. In 1963, and again in 1967, Cage had organized marathon performances of *Vexations* (1893), a peculiar little piece that Satie had indicated should be played 840 times in succession. Two decades earlier, Cage had made an arrangement for two pianos of the first part of Satie's three-movement drama *Socrate* (1918); this was used as the accompaniment to Cunningham's 1947 solo dance *Idyllic Song*. Possibly prompted by the 1967 performance of *Vexations*, in the following year Cage arranged the remaining two parts of *Socrate* for two pianos, for which Cunningham made two new ensemble dances. The entire work was scheduled for performance in 1970, but at the end of 1969 Satie's publisher—Editions Max Eschig—refused permission for the use of the arrangement. Cage's entirely pragmatic response was to make a new piece "with the rhythms and phrases of *Socrate*, but with the pitches so altered that he could stay clear of any copyright problems."[9] The new piece was—equally pragmatically—called *Cheap Imitation*, and Cunningham's dance was accordingly titled *Second Hand*.

The principal difference between *Cheap Imitation* and Cage's original two-piano arrangement of *Socrate* is that while the latter includes all of Satie's music, the former is derived only from its (mainly vocal) melodic line; it is thus monophonic. Subsequently, "becoming attached to the imitation as I had for many years been attached to the original,"[10] Cage made arrangements of *Cheap Imitation* for an orchestra of between twenty-four and ninety-five players (1972), and later for solo violin (1977). The chance-derived orchestral version is of particular interest for Cage's instruction that "those who play are to seat themselves together in any unconventional way: not according to instrumental categories. . . . The orchestra's conductor will help the musicians in the preparation of a performance, using *Cheap Imitation, Piano Solo.*"[11] Also of note is Cage's requirement for a minimum rehearsal schedule lasting two weeks: this was a result not so much of his earlier experiences with the New York Philharmonic Orchestra but rather of the severely under-rehearsed premiere of *Cheap Imitation*, given in The Hague in May 1972. Indeed, Cage was forced to cancel what was subsequently promised as the first complete performance—at the Holland Festival a few weeks later—for similar reasons:

> [I] told the musicians what I thought about the deplorable state of the society in which we live—not just musical society. . . . I congratulated myself for having come up with, in the composition of *Cheap Imitation,* something capable of opening the ears of orchestra musicians. I had offered them something with which to make music, and not, as is practiced today, something with which to scrape together a little money.
>
> I am convinced that they play the music of others as badly as mine. However . . . one must take care not to reproach individuals for that absence of devotion—whether they be musicians or simple vacationers throwing their garbage in the streams. We must hold the present organization of society responsible for this. That is the raison d'etre of revolution.[12]

As with his New York Philharmonic experience, what Cage seems to have abhorred here was the musicians' lack of discipline, and it was by no means the last time he encountered such behavior.[13]

An obvious source for Cage's mention in this passage of revolution was the life and work of Mao Tse-tung; indeed, in the foreword to *M: Writings '67–'72*, Cage writes at length on Mao, as well as noting at the outset that while the title of the book "was obtained by subjecting the twenty-six letters of the alphabet to an I Ching chance operation . . . M is, to be sure, the first letter of many words and names that have concerned me for many years (music, mushrooms, Marcel Duchamp, M. C. Richards, Morris Graves, Mark Tobey, Merce Cunningham, Marshall McLuhan, my dear friends the Daniels—Minna, for twenty-three years the editor of *Modern Music*, and Mell, early in life and now again in later life, the painter), and recently (mesostics, Mao Tse-tung)."[14] Cage's somewhat naive enthusiasm for Mao was short-lived; more importantly, though, M was also "the first letter of *Mureau* . . . [which is] the first syllable of the word music followed by the second of the name Thoreau." If *Cheap Imitation* marked a new beginning in Cage's music, then his engagement with the life and work of Henry David Thoreau (1817–62) marked a new beginning in Cage's philosophical and aesthetic outlook.[15]

Although he had read Thoreau's *On the Duty of Civil Disobedience* as a student, Cage only really became aware of his work in 1967, through the poet Wendell Berry.[16] Two facets of Thoreau's philosophy—his love of nature and his dislike of regimentation—seem particularly to have appealed to Cage, who must have responded with empathy to these lines from *Walden*: "If a man does not keep pace with his companions, perhaps it is because he hears a different drummer. Let him step to the music which he hears, however measured or far away." Thus, specifically in the first half of the 1970s, but also more generally for the remainder of his life, Cage was inspired by Thoreau's example in a number of new works. In music, the most obvious manifestations of this are to be found in *Song Books (Solos for Voice 3–92)* (1970) and *Score (40 Drawings by Thoreau) and 23 Parts* (1974) for any instruments. As its title suggests, *Song Books* was the extended successor to two shorter, earlier works: *Solo for Voice 1* (1958) grew out of the instrumental parts of the *Concert for Piano and Orchestra*, while *Solo for Voice 2* (1960), for one or more voices, is one of the pieces based in the use of musical tools. If the *Concert's Solo for Piano* had been a vast compendium of compositional possibilities for the keyboard, then *Song Books* achieves the same end for the voice. It consists of 317 pages, which contain over fifty different types of composition. In a manner analogous to that found in the *Solo for Piano*, some of the compositional types of *Song Books* replicate earlier styles—whether derived from *Winter Music* or *Aria*—while others open up new directions, such as the pairing of music with theater. In notational terms, there are quasi-pictorial materials (including a portrait of Thoreau and a map of his hometown of Concord, Massachusetts), pitch curves like those that had been used in *Aria*, point-drawing techniques similar to those found in *Atlas Eclipticalis*, and even conventional stave writing. There are also imitations of Satie's writing, which are related to those of *Cheap Imitation*. But despite this stylistic profusion—which is symptomatic of the sense of "accepting" abundance that characterizes Cage's work of this period—all ninety of the new *Solos for Voice* have a common link, for Cage used chance operations to determine whether or not each should be related to a single idea ("We connect Satie with Thoreau") that had first appeared in the 1969 installment (part V) of the "Diary: How to Improve the World (You Will Only Make Matters Worse)."[17] Interestingly, given

another aspect of Cage's work that was shortly to emerge—his extended involvement with James Joyce's *Finnegans Wake*—the specific context for the connecting
thread in *Song Books* is

> Whole
> Earth. We connect Satie with Thoreau.
> Eleventh thunderclap?

a composite reference to McLuhan, Satie, Thoreau, and the ten hundred-letter
words found in Joyce's novel. In *Song Books*, the *I Ching* was also used to determine
two other facets of each solo: first, whether it was a song, a song using electronics,
theater, or theater using electronics; and second, its basic compositional method.
The end result is one of enormous diversity and richness, impossible to define in
conventional terms. As Cage put it, "[T]o consider the *Song Books* as a work of art
is nearly impossible. Who would dare? It resembles a brothel, doesn't it?"[18]

Unlike the *Song Books*, Cage's second Thoreau work—the *Score (40 Drawings by Thoreau) and 23 Parts*—is not an example of the kind of uncoordinated
ensemble performance that had characterized such pieces as the *Concert*. Instead,
in *Score*, forty drawings taken from Thoreau's handwritten *Journal* were placed
randomly onto twelve staff-systems, the "score" of the title. Each of these systems is arranged in seventeen units, structured—like the Japanese poetic *haiku*—
as 5 : 7 : 5. Chance operations determined the orchestration of the drawings
as the twenty-three instrumental parts, as well as other features relating to
their performance. However, a rendition of *Score* does not consist solely of the
twelve staff-systems; rather, each of these is followed by a silence of approximately equal length, and the piece is concluded by a recording of the dawn at
Stony Point (made on August 6, 1974) that is of the same approximate length
as everything that has preceded it.[19] Closely related to *Score* is *Renga* (1976) for
seventy-eight instruments or voices: here, 361 of Thoreau's drawings are used,
and the structure is derived from that of the Japanese *renga*. (A *renga* consists
of at least thirty-six *wakas*, short poems whose syllabic structure is 5 : 7 : 5 : 7 :
7.) As Cage describes the score, "Vertical space gives relative pitch within limits
determined by the performer. . . . Horizontal space gives conducted time."[20] The
I Ching was used to determine the placement of the Thoreau drawings within
the (score) structure, which was then "taken apart" to make the seventy-eight
parts. Instruments are not specified, permitting "the use of instruments from
other cultures and times." As with *Score*, but less rigidly, "[T]he conductor may
introduce silences at the ends of most of the lines"; the conductor additionally
determines the (changing) tempi.[21] Also related to *Score* (and thence *Renga*) is

Ryoanji (1983–85), a series of pieces whose graphic scores, while resembling those of the Thoreau-derived works, were created by drawing around rocks.[22]

Renga, which had been commissioned by Seiji Ozawa and the Boston Symphony Orchestra, is usually coupled in performance with *Apartment House 1776* (1976), a mixed-media event (or musicircus) for any ensemble. The work was one of the pieces Cage wrote in response to the occasion of the bicentennial of the American Declaration of Independence. Unsurprisingly, it took a somewhat oblique view of that event: Cage wished to "do something with early American music that would let it keep its flavor at the same time that it would lose what was so obnoxious to me: its harmonic tonality."[23] Accordingly, he used chance techniques to select forty-four early American choral pieces by such composers as William Billings, Andrew Law, and the bizarrely named Supply Belcher. Then, using a technique he termed "subtraction," Cage systematically extended certain pitches from each of the original vocal lines, while simultaneously removing those other pitches that should have intervened, before following each extended pitch with a similarly extended silence. In Cage's words, "[T]he cadences and everything disappeared; but the flavor remained. You can recognize it as eighteenth-century music, but it's suddenly brilliant in a new way. It is because each sound vibrates from itself, not from a theory. . . . The cadences which were the function of the theory, to make syntax and all, all of this is gone; so that you get the most marvelous overlappings."[24] The resulting recompositions are added to a *mélange* that also includes eighteenth-century popular melodies, drum solos, and Moravian church music, together with live or recorded vocal solos "representing four of the people who lived here two hundred years ago—the American Indian, the Sephardic Jew, the Negro slave, and the Protestants. . . . So you have a situation that can't be considered an object but rather resembles an environment."[25] Processes of subtraction are also found in a number of other pieces from this time, including *Quartets I–VIII* for small orchestra (1976) or twelve amplified voices and symphonic band (1978), *Some of "The Harmony of Maine"* (1978) for organ(ist) with three to six assistants, and *Hymns and Variations* (1979) for twelve amplified voices.

Another major bicentennial commission, this time from the Canadian Broadcasting Corporation, also drew on Thoreau. *Lecture on the Weather* (1975), for twelve voices and tape, opens with an overtly political preface that criticizes the legal system and the government (among other equally deserving targets) before explaining that in the piece, Cage wanted "to give another opportunity for us, whether of one nation or another, to examine again, as Thoreau continually did, ourselves, both as individuals and as members of society, and the world in which we live."[26] The preface concludes by repeating part of the dedication of *A Year from Monday* and *M:* that "the U.S.A. may become just another part of the world, no more, no less." *Lecture on the Weather* proper, which uses the same structural proportions as *4' 33"*, consists of three elements: the first is the collage text delivered by twelve speaker-vocalists, or speaker-instrumentalists, which was obtained by subjecting various of Thoreau's writings—including the *Journal*, *Walden*, and *On the Duty of Civil Disobedience*—to *I Ching* chance operations. Cage specifies that the declaimers of these texts should preferably be "American men who had become Canadian citizens"—in other words, draft-dodgers.[27] The second element is an array of recordings, made by Maryanne Amacher, of wind and rain. And in the literally thunderous final section of the work, the recordings are joined by the third element, "a film by Luis Frangella representing lightning by means of briefly projected negatives of Thoreau's drawings."[28]

Just as *Apartment House 1776* is associated with a group of smaller "satellite" works based on subtraction techniques, so might *Score (40 Drawings by Thoreau) and 23 Parts*, *Renga*, and *Lecture on the Weather* be seen as having a cluster of satellite pieces, all concerned in some way with nature. Among these pieces are *Bird Cage* (1972) for twelve tapes; *Child of Tree* (1975) and *Branches* (1976) for amplified plant materials; *Inlets (Improvisation II)* (1977) for four performers with conch shells and the sound of fire; *49 Waltzes for the Five Boroughs* (1977) and *A Dip in the Lake* (1978); and *Litany for the Whale* (1980) for two voices. The antepenultimate and penultimate works in this list are of particular note: the first was intended for performance in New York City and the second in Chicago, and in each case the concept is "to go to places and either listen to, perform at and/or make a recording of the sounds and therefore possibly connect with the life of a city."[29] Also related to this nature group are *Etcetera* (1973) for small orchestra, tape, and three conductors and *Etcetera 2 / 4 Orchestras* (1985) for orchestra and tape, in that each calls for a recording "made in Cage's own composing environments (Stony Point and his New York loft)."[30]

One other group of works from the 1970s and 1980s—the three sets of *Etudes*—is essentially unconnected to the various threads identified so far in this chapter. Despite their somewhat abstract nature, however, these pieces establish firm links with two of Cage's earlier preoccupations, virtuosity and star maps. By the 1970s, David Tudor had become more of a composer than a performer, and so Cage was no longer able to utilize his particular brand of virtuosity as a spur to creation. Other virtuosi, though, queued up to commission new works from Cage; and in each case he responded by writing sets of quasi-nineteenth-century miniatures, designed to exploit and extend the instrumental capabilities of the commissioner. As Cage put it in 1989, "I wanted to make the music as difficult as possible so that a performance would show that the impossible is not impossible."[31] Furthermore, all three sets of *Etudes* were composed using star maps, recalling Cage's earlier practice in such works as *Atlas Eclipticalis* and some of the *Solos for Voice 3–92*.

The thirty-two *Etudes Australes* (1974–75) for piano were written at the request of Grete Sultan, whom Cage had known since the period he spent studying with Richard Buhlig in the early 1930s. According to Cage, the title "comes from *Atlas Australis*, a book of star maps printed in six colors . . . published in Czechoslovakia. In order to write one of the 32 two-page pieces, I began by placing a transparent grid over a particular one of the 24 maps. *Etude I* is derived from Maps XXIV and XXIII."[32] The *I Ching* was consulted to answer various questions relating to—for example—the number of stars to be traced, and of which color. The actual music consists of single notes and chords. Cage created a table of all the possible chords that could be played at the piano by each of Sultan's hands, and over the course of the thirty-two etudes the number of chords per etude increases incrementally. One result of Cage's compositional method was that in performance, Sultan's hands were frequently required to cross. As a whole, *Etudes Australes* has an austere beauty; and like much contemporaneous minimalist music, its true impact can only be felt over a whole performance, as the density of the music gradually increases.

The *Freeman Etudes* (1977–80; 1989–90) for violin—commissioned by the prominent West Coast patron Betty Freeman—were written for, and with considerable input from, Paul Zukovsky and subsequently Irvine Arditti. Again, the complete set consists of thirty-two miniatures and is dauntingly virtuosic. The chance operations employed here were even more complex than those that had generated the *Music of Changes*; indeed, Cage stopped composing the set after he had written number eighteen, convinced that the music was unplayable. Almost a decade later, "he decided to add the performance indication that the violinist, when faced with an impossible density of notes, should simply play as many as possible."[33] Similar difficulties arose with the *Etudes Boreales* (1978) for cello and piano. Written at the request of Jack and Jeanne Kirstein, the commissioners found the pieces unplayable, and it fell to Frances-Marie Utti and Michael Pugliese (the latter, ironically, a virtuoso percussionist) to give the premieres. Although presented as a duo, the two sets of *Etudes Boreales*—for cello and piano—were written separately, and can be performed either as solos or together. Cage likened their relationship to that of "the music and dance in the theatre of Merce Cunningham."[34]

There is a final "new beginning" of the 1970s that requires comment; for although it was unrelated in any specific sense to Cage's work, it was nevertheless fundamental to his ability to undertake that work. Cage's health had been in decline throughout the 1960s. Plagued by arthritis and other problems, by 1972 his wrists "were so swollen . . . that he could no longer pick up a glass with one hand."[35] The toes of his left foot were completely numb, and his teeth were causing him trouble; he was taking a dozen aspirin every day. Help came eventually via Yoko Ono, whom Cage had known for many years, initially as the spouse of his student Toshi Ichiyanagi. Ono told Cage that he must go "'to Shizuko Yamomoto [who will] change your diet and give you Shiatsu massage.'"[36] This remark chimed in with comments that had been made by Cage's astrologer, Julie Winter, and by a Chinese doctor in Paris. On Yamomoto's advice, Cage stopped smoking and drinking and ate only those foods specified by the macrobiotic diet. Within a few months he was much better, and in 1979 (aged sixty-seven) he could declare that "since this change I think I've been more active than I've been since 1952."[37] However, while the changes in Cage's lifestyle improved his general health, they could not prevent him aging. During his last decade he suffered from several complaints common among the elderly, including sciatica and arteriosclerosis. In 1985 he broke his left arm; and around the same time he experienced the first of several strokes, the last of which led to his death.

Writings Through

Just as Cage's discovery of Thoreau's work resulted in an outpouring of musical creativity, so too did it lead to a new wave of writings. The first of these was "Mureau" (1970), published in *M*, which Cage describes as "one of the more unconventional texts in [the] book."[38] Created by "subjecting all the remarks of . . . Thoreau about music, silence, and sounds he heard that are in the Dover publication of the *Journal* to a series of I Ching operations," the text is "a mix of letters, syllables, words, phrases, and sentences."[39] Until this point, Cage's writings—even though many of them were made using procedures analogous to those employed in his compositions—had generally followed the standard laws of syntax; but "Mureau" "departs from conventional syntax" and as such represents an important development in Cage's work.[40] As he notes in the foreword to *M*, "[S]yntax, according to Norman O. Brown, is the arrangement of the army. As we move away from it, we demilitarize language. This demilitarization of language is conducted in many ways: a single language is pulverized [as in "Mureau"]; the boundaries between two or more languages are crossed [as had occurred in the text of *Aria*, back in 1958]; elements not strictly linguistic (graphic, musical) are introduced; etc. Translation becomes, if not impossible, unnecessary. Nonsense and silence are produced, familiar to lovers. We begin to actually live together, and the thought of separating doesn't enter our minds."[41]

Cage also notes here that "My work in this field is tardy," having been preceded by the poetry of his former student Jackson MacLow, as well as in more general terms by the efforts of concrete and sound poets. As was so often the case, having identified something in his life or work that he perceived as lacking, Cage set out to rectify it. Thus much of his writing after "Mureau" is equally—though often differently—demilitarized. This is certainly true of a second major text derived from Thoreau, the quadripartite "Empty Words" (1973–75), which is printed complete in *Empty Words: Writings '73–'78*.[42] Each of the four parts of the main text is preceded by a short contextualizing introduction. Cage saw "Empty Words" as a continuation of "Mureau," but "extending it beyond Thoreau's remarks about sound and music to the whole of the *Journal*."[43] He had been told that Chinese could be "classified into 'full words' and 'empty words.'"[44] A full word is a noun, verb, adjective, or adverb; an empty word is a connective or pronoun—"a word that refers to something else."[45] In a manner analogous to (but in reverse of) the chordal accumulation that characterizes the complete set of *Etudes Australes*, in "Empty Words" the text gradually dissembles. "As we start Lecture One . . . we have no sentences. Though they did exist in *Mureau*, now they've gone. In the second [lecture], the phrases are gone, and in the third part the words are gone, except those that have only one syllable. And in the last one, everything is gone but letters and silences."[46] Thus "Empty Words" as a whole moves from its relatively meaningful opening lines

        notAt evening
            right can see
                suited to the morning hour

                trucksrsq Measured tSee t A
        ys sfOi w dee e str oais

to the meaningless, but no less beautiful, closing passage

                th r du
                o t lde
            s e l tho
    te   ee
        e   rthr rH i nd
                dwh dpl e

tmdprl rt,

thltht shh swh e atveth mf *d*n nd e aie

ean byo odo.[47]

"Mureau" had been conceived as a printed text, though Cage had taken to vocalizing it in performance during the early 1970s. Conversely, "Empty Words" was conceived as a performance piece (with each of its four parts lasting two and a half hours), but is better known in its printed form. Unsurprisingly, Cage discovered that "[m]ost people consider this [length] excessive, and they don't want me to give it as a lecture."[48] However, given the intention that a complete reading of the piece "starts during the evening, and terminates at dawn, with the sound of waking birds being heard,"[49] one might argue that reservations concerning the oral delivery of "Empty Words" are short-sighted: its cumulative effect over ten hours, with the climax occurring with "the opening of the doors to the outer world so that the sounds would come in," would probably be stunning and would suitably match Cage's aspirations for the work as "a transition from literature to music."[50] One other aspect of the printed version of the text requires comment: in the foreword to *M*, Cage identified one of the means by which language might be demilitarized to be the inclusion of "elements not strictly linguistic (graphic, musical)." In "Empty Words," this is achieved by the chance-determined placement throughout the text of Thoreau's drawings, used almost as ideograms— "character[s] symbolizing the idea of a thing without expressing its name."[51]

There are other Cage texts influenced by, or derived from, the work of Thoreau—such as "Song" and "Another Song"[52]—but one stands out as a useful interface with two other aspects of Cage's literary work. *Essay* (for tape; 1987) is the short title of *Writings through the Essay: On the Duty of Civil Disobedience*, a work intended in part as an installation and in part as the accompaniment to Cunningham's dance *Points in Space*. The basic text of *Essay* was written as a series of mesostics, a poetic form invented by Cage in which a key word or phrase runs down not the left-hand margin of the text (as in an acrostic) but rather down the middle. A simple mesostic appears in the colophon to this book. In the case of *Essay*, the text is derived from Thoreau's *On the Duty of Civil Disobedience*, but the key phrase running down its center is the title of a work by Satie, *Messe des Pauvres* (1893–95). An example of this combination is given in *John Cage: Writer*:

Man will

useEful

man will not Submit

to leaSt

throughout thE

worlD

   hE who
  himSelf entirely

    Put through
    And
with retUrn

    priVate feelings
    foR
    thE
proportion aS[53]

Mesostics of various kinds dominate Cage's literary output from 1970 onwards: the first, "written as prose to celebrate one of Edwin Denby's birthdays," appears in *M.*[54] Most are printed conventionally, though the "62 Mesostics re Merce Cunningham"—which "resemble waterfalls or ideograms"—are rendered in a huge array of chance-determined typefaces and sizes.[55] The main feature that determines the wording of a given mesostic (or mesostic series) is that "a given letter capitalized does not occur between it and the preceding capitalized letter."[56] However, in 1979 Louis Mink pointed out to Cage that "a pure mesostic . . . would not permit the appearance of either letter between two of the name."[57] This led to some procedural revisions in Cage's subsequent mesostics.

One vital development that enabled Cage to produce so much new work in the last two decades of his life was his use of computer programs of various kinds. For *HPSCHD* (1967–69), Lejaren Hiller and his team devised a number of programs to generate the fifty-one tapes, each of which used "a different division of the octave, ranging from five to fifty-six tones (excluding the standard twelve-note division)."[58] Other programs were employed to produce the music for two of the seven harpsichords, and one program in particular—written by Ed Kobrin—produced a printed stack of *I Ching* hexagrams. This "automation" (to use William Brooks's word) of Cage's compositional processes revolutionized his working practices, removing the need for time-consuming consultations of the *I Ching* using the more traditional method of tossing coins or yarrow sticks. All Cage had to do was to refer on the printout to "the next available hexagram, then [cross] it out."[59] Some of the other musical uses of computer programs in Cage's work will be discussed below; but in terms of his writings, they allowed the rapid creation of (draft) mesostics from any source text that was fed into the computer's memory. As Cage put it in another context, "Technology essentially is a way of getting more done with less effort."[60]

Among the more substantial examples of Cage's mesostic-based writings of the 1970s are "62 Mesostics re Merce Cunningham" (1970–71), "36 Mesostics Re and Not Re Marcel Duchamp" (1972), and "25 Mesostics Re and Not Re Mark Tobey" (ca. 1972) (all in *M*); "Sixty-One Mesostics Re and Not Re Norman O. Brown" (1977; in *Empty Words*); the majority of "James Joyce, Marcel Duchamp, Erik Satie: An Alphabet" (1979) and "Composition in Retrospect" (first version, 1981) (both in *X*). However, by far the most sustained example of Cage's mesostic art was derived from a book that he had loved since the time of its publication—and which he considered "the most important book of the twentieth century"[61]—but, at least in the Cagean mythology, he never read in its entirety: James Joyce's 1939 classic, *Finnegans Wake*.

The first installment of Cage's "Writing through Finnegans Wake" dates from 1976 and consists of 115 pages of mesostics. He characterized the undertaking as "a discipline similar to that of counterpoint in music with a cantus firmus."[62] When his editor at Wesleyan University Press suggested that the end product was too long, Cage wrote a new series of mesostics, following a more rigid method, titled "Writing for the Second Time through Finnegans Wake" (1977).[63] Subsequently, other approaches yielded "Writing for the Third Time through Finnegans Wake" (1979; unpublished), "Writing for the Fourth Time through Finnegans Wake" (1980), and "Muoyce (Writing for the Fifth Time through Finnegans Wake)" (1980).[64] This last, which is not in mesostic form, was described by Cage as being "with respect to *Finnegans Wake* what *Mureau* was with respect to the *Journal* of Henry David Thoreau."[65] Cage saw the various "Writings through Finnegans Wake" as being, in part, "that of identifying, as Duchamp had, found objects." But elsewhere, "I found myself from time to time bursting into laughter. . . . The play of sex and church and food and drink in an all time all space world turned family was not only regaling; it Joyced me."[66]

There was also a musical by-product of the "Writings through Finnegans Wake" series: Cage was invited by Klaus Schöning of WDR Cologne to "write music to accompany a broadcast" of "Writing for the Second Time through Finnegans Wake."[67] The result was the multimedia work *Roaratorio* (1979). *Roaratorio*'s principal elements are the reading of "Writing for the Second Time through Finnegans Wake," which can be live or via the tape made by Cage; the live performance of Irish traditional music by a singer, piper, fiddler, flutist, and one or two bodhran players; and a composite tape of the huge array of sounds and music referred to in Joyce's book. An optional element is dance, provided by the Cunningham Dance Company. The tape of Cage's reading "served as the template for the placement of the other recorded sounds. . . . Thus the piece opens with the sound of a viola d'amore ('Sir Tristram, violes d'amores, fr'over the short sea') and closes with the cries of gulls ('Whish! A gull. Gulls. Far calls. Coming, far!').”[68] Specific characteristics of each of the sounds—such as their loudness and duration—were identified by chance operations, as were the timings of the live musicians' appearances. The whole work can be performed live—as a later incarnation of the musicircus concept—or be experienced as a recording. Finally, in a manner analogous to that of *Fontana Mix*, the general processes used to create *Roaratorio* can be applied to any literary work: this metaversion of the piece is titled “_____, _____ *Circus on* _____,” where “the first blank is the title (here *Roaratorio*), the second an article and an adjective (*an Irish* in this case), and the last the title of the book from which it is drawn”[69]—hence the full title of the original piece becomes *Roaratorio, an Irish Circus on Finnegans Wake*.

Visual Art

The 1958 Stable Gallery exhibit of some of his scores had seen the rebirth of Cage's career as a visual artist; subsequently, there were other public displays of his musical calligraphy, such as those in Rhode Island and Milan in 1971 and that associated with *Renga* at New York's Museum of Modern Art in 1977.[70] And back in 1969, with the assistance of Calvin Sumsion, Cage had made the two lithographs and eight plexigrams collectively titled *Not Wanting to Say Anything about Marcel*. In 1977, he was invited by Kathan Brown to work with the printers at Crown Point Press (then located in Oakland, California) on some etchings. Perhaps surprisingly, given his devotion to music and the already copious demands on his time, Cage accepted: his reason for doing so, as he explained to Brown, was that he "had once received an invitation from a friend [Geeta Sarabhai] to walk with her in the Himalayas, and he had not accepted. 'I have always regretted this,' he added."[71] Neither Brown nor Cage could have anticipated that, over the next fourteen years (mainly at Crown Point Press, but also at the Mountain Lake Workshop in Virginia and at home in New York) Cage would produce almost 950 separate works of art, including prints, drawings, and watercolors.[72]

Just as Cage's writings since the late 1940s had been intrinsically linked with the processes used to create his music, so too were his prints, drawings, and watercolors. As Kathan Brown has put it, "Cage worked with visual art in almost the same way he worked with music. His printers or assistants were something like musicians—he developed scores for them to execute. The printers were indispensable, but this was not collaborative work—the vision was his; he was the artist."[73] The specific techniques employed in each series of artworks are described in detail in Brown's *John Cage — Visual Art: To Sober and Quiet the Mind*, as well as in her chapter in *The Cambridge Companion to John Cage*. No duplication of those descriptions is needed here, but it is appropriate to focus on one group of images to illustrate the kinds of method Cage employed.

Between 1978 and 1982, Cage produced several sets of prints at Crown Point Press, including *Score without Parts (40 Drawings by Thoreau): Twelve Haiku* (1978), *Seven Day Diary (Without Knowing)* (1978), *Signals* (1978), *Changes and Disappearances* (1979–82), *On the Surface* (1980–82), and *Déreau* (1982). In 1983, however, Cage turned to drawing—both directly on paper and by using a sharp drypoint tool on copper plates. The resulting body of work is collectively titled *Ryoanji* (cf. the musical compositions for various forces from 1983–85[74]), in reference to the Ryoanji garden in Kyoto, which dates from circa 1490. Cage visited this Zen garden in 1962 and was impressed by its natural simplicity: "[A] flat plain of raked sand, with five clutches of stones rising from nests of moss; two groups of two stones, two groups of three, one group of five."[75] Stones therefore became the subject matter of the *Ryoanji* series: when he arrived at Crown Point Press in January 1983, Cage brought with him a bag of "sixteen of them, each two to three inches across."[76] From the sixteen stones, Cage selected fifteen (the number in the Ryoanji garden) and for the prints located each stone—via chance operations—on a single test plate, using a variant of the grid coordinate system he had employed in his earlier prints. He then drew around the stones, scratching lines into the copper plates with the sharp drypoint tool. The series title is *Where R=Ryoanji*, with the character R equating to the number 15. Each individual work has a shorthand subtitle that describes the exact process used: $2R+13 \cdot (13 \cdot 14)14$, for instance, indicates that Cage "drew around two stones fifteen times each [2R], then [+] drew around thirteen stones fourteen times each [$13 \cdot (13 \cdot 14)14$]."[77] Similarly, $R^2 2$ is one of three prints based on the fifteen rocks [R] each being drawn around 225 times [^{2}]; the final 2 refers to the use of medium drawing pressure. The print series was completed by two prints based on R being cubed; but there is also a further series of drawings that were made directly onto paper, using pencils. Here, Cage used chance to determine which pencils, from a selection running from 6B to 9H, were to be used. A typical subtitle in this series is $R8/15$, meaning that "there are fifteen times eight stone tracings done with fifteen different pencils."[78]

Indian Summer

Having reached the age of sixty-five in 1977, Cage began to think of retirement: he mentioned to Cunningham that if he moved to—for instance—Bolivia, "the cost of living there would mean he could exist frugally on what he had already earned."[79] Cunningham's response is not recorded. However, as a result of its reincarnation in 1953 as the Avenue of the Americas, the lampposts on Sixth Avenue had been adorned with decorative plaques, each bearing the name of a different American country. One day, looking out of their apartment window, Cage noticed that the plaque on the lamppost opposite celebrated Bolivia. Retirement from creativity, though, was far from Cage's mind; indeed, during the last decade of his life—a veritable Indian Summer—he produced a huge amount of new material, including over eighty compositions, numerous writings (some of them of major length), twelve series of artworks, a film (*One*[11] [1991]), and a touring exhibition (*Rolywholyover: A Circus* [1992]).

One important factor in this context was the degree to which automation could help in "getting more done with less effort." The *I Ching* hexagram printouts—now generated by a new program written by Andrew Culver—were employed across Cage's creative spectrum, but other software applications assisted with more specific tasks. Cage's writings were considerably aided by two programs—Mesomake and Mesolist—written in the mid- to late 1980s by Jim Rosenberg. The mesostic series that resulted from these programs include "Writing through 'Howl'" (1986), "Three Mesostics" (1986), "Sports" (1989), and "Mirakus: *Mirage*

John Cage with Sidney Robertson Cowell (widow of Henry Cowell), at the Windfall Dutch Barn at Salt Springsville, New York, summer 1983. Photograph by John Mazarak. Courtesy of John Mazarak.

Verbal" (1990);[80] "Anarchy" (1988);[81] "Themes and Variations" (1980);[82] and especially *I–VI* (1988).

I–VI—or, to give it its full title, *MethodStructureIntentionDisciplineNotation-
IndeterminacyInterpenetrationImitationDevotionCircumstancesVariableStructureNon-
understandingContingencyInconsistencyPerformance*—is the senary text delivered at
Harvard University in 1988–89, when Cage was Charles Eliot Norton Professor of Poetry.[83] (Previous incumbents of the post include Aaron Copland, T. S.
Eliot, and Igor Stravinsky.) Cage's six lectures, together with his introduction,
the source text, and a transcription of the associated seminar series, occupy 452
large pages in their published form. The source text itself—which Cage sometimes referred to as the "Bolivia Mix"[84]—was created by making chance selections from Thoreau's *Walden*, L. C. Beckett's *Neti Neti*, Cage's own "Composition
in Retrospect," writings by Emerson, Wittgenstein, McLuhan, and Fuller, and
several newspapers. The mesostic spine running down the center of *I–VI* is the
fifteen-word composite that gives the work its proper title. As chance determined
not only the nature and content of the source text but also various aspects of its
rendition in mesostic form, the lectures in delivery made even less conventional
sense than usual. This is apparent from the short mesostic that appears on the
first page of the first lecture:

                    the rule My
                         th**E** '
                    cu**T**backs would not
        it misled   **H**im '
                    l**O**ng time **what** '
        place to place ' but **D**oes it look[85]

Consequently, the lectures became performances, for as Andrew Culver has noted,
Cage had—over the previous several years—voluntarily or of necessity given up
performing as a pianist and percussionist and as music director of the Cunningham Dance Company. Therefore, "all he had left was text reading."[86] Incidentally,
Cage's appointment as Charles Eliot Norton Professor was but one of a series of
honors he received in his later years. For instance, in 1966 he was made a Knight
of Mark Twain; in 1968 he was elected to the National Institute of Arts and Letters and in 1978 to a Fellowship of the American Academy of Arts and Sciences;
in 1980 he was Regents Lecturer at the University of California at San Diego;
and in 1986 he was awarded the honorary degree of Doctor of All the Arts by
the California Institute of the Arts.

Probably the most significant impact of the automation of Cage's working practices occurred in relation to his music. Between 1983 and 1988, Andrew Culver worked as his full-time computing assistant and continued part-time in that role until Cage's death. Culver wrote around twenty-five separate programs for Cage:[87] some were quite specific in their uses—for instance, Chairbar (1991) generated the chair positions for an installation of *Essay* in Barcelona—but others had more general applications. Since 1981, in *Thirty Pieces for Five Orchestras*, Cage had been using flexible time brackets, whereby each musical "action" is placed between given start and end times; however, these start and end times are themselves flexible. Here is an abstract example:

0' 00" ↔ 0' 45"   [musical action]   0' 30" ↔ 1' 15"

The start time of the action can be at any point between 0' 00" and 0' 45"; and its end time can be at any point between 0' 30" and 1' 15". The action in itself could be silence; a single note surrounded by rests; a complex series of gestures; or any other possibility lying between these extremes. Thus, in the flexible time-bracket system, musical actions "can 'float' in the brackets allotted to them . . . [with] the unused portion of the time bracket . . . left silent."[88] The impetus for the procedure used in *Thirty Pieces for Five Orchestras* had come from the methods employed in the creation of the print series *On the Surface* (1980–82); but in a broader sense, Cage had discovered, in David Revill's words, a way of "multiplying simple means to reach a complex solution. He had found a new, lighter, more economical way to achieve the multiplicity he sought."[89] (In his time-bracket scores Cage also, coincidentally, returns to a relatively determinate compositional process and a relatively conventional notational practice.) Further examples of the flexible time-bracket approach are found in such works as *Thirty Pieces for String Quartet* (1983) and the ongoing *Music for* (1984–87).[90] However, from approximately 1986 onwards, the automation of the creation of time brackets (as well as their contents)—via a number of programs written by Culver—hugely increased Cage's output, leading to the *Europeras* and the so-called number pieces.

The idea of the iconoclast John Cage writing an opera might seem unlikely, yet between 1987 and 1991 he wrote five. However, as with everything else that Cage was involved in, his operas are in no sense conventional. The original invitation to write *Europeras 1 and 2* (1987), for nineteen voices, twenty-one players, and tape, had come from Heinz-Klaus Metzger and Rainer Riehn. Cage saw the works as carrying "the independence but coexistence of music and dance with which Cunningham and I were familiar, to all the elements of theatre, including the lighting, program booklets, decors, properties, costumes, and stage action."[91] More mischievously—and perhaps in part finally getting his revenge on Europe for the treatment it had afforded him in the 1950s—Cage also remarked, "'For two hundred years the Europeans have been sending us their operas. Now I'm sending them back.'"[92]

As might be surmised from the first of these comments, each of the principal facets of the *Europeras* was composed independently, an undertaking that would have been unthinkable without the computer programs devised by Culver. As James Tenney has noted, "[W]ould Cage have lived long enough to have realized *Europeras* if he'd had to do it the old way? I don't think so. The technology made possible some large-scale projects that he otherwise would never have thought of embarking on."[93] The vocalists were instructed to select arias from eighteenth- and nineteenth-century operas and to sing them within specific, chance-determined time frames; the instrumental parts were culled, using the time-bracket system, from the accompaniments to other public-domain operatic works. In addition to the vocal and instrumental layers, there were sporadic interruptions from a "truckera": these consisted in "a few seconds' snatch of a three-minute tape consisting of a forty-eight track stack of chance selections from recordings of traditional opera." The effect was "'as if you were shouting to someone on the opposite side of the street and a large truck passes by.'"[94] Costumes were chosen randomly by the singers, but "sets, lighting, props, and stage directions were all designed using chance" as a result of Culver's programs titled Flatcues, Imagecue, and Lightcues.[95] However, as in *Theatre Piece* (1960), Cage was careful to avoid—as he put it in the instructions for that earlier piece—"physically dangerous obstacles that may arise due to the unpredictability involved." The final element in this deliberately chaotic confection—designed as much to confuse as to illuminate those attending—was the provision of randomly distributed (chance-created) synopses, "one per program, so that different members of the audience had different narratives to follow."[96]

If *Europeras 1 and 2* are in the tradition of grand opera, then *Europeras 3 and 4* (1990), for six voices, two pianists, twelve Victrolas, and tape, and *Europera 5* (1991), for two voices, piano, Victrola, and tape/TV/radio, are chamber operas. The basic format—of disparate live arias and accompaniments, placed in unrelated settings—is the same; but now Cage added a further dimension, via the Victrola phonographs, of carefully selected recordings from the opera back catalog. Their function—while superficially similar to that of the recordings in *Credo in Us* (1942), *Imaginary Landscape No. 5* (1952), and so on—is to connect not only with the history of opera (as happens in *Europeras 1 and 2*) but also with its performance history. As David Revill puts it, "[T]he voices of Cage's youth, or young manhood, now long-dead, crackle out at us across the years in a decentered chorus."[97]

The collective moniker "number pieces" has been usefully applied by James Pritchett to the large final group of Cage's works—dating from 1987 through 1992—whose titles share the same basic characteristic of simply announcing the number of their performers (e.g., *Two* [1987] for flute and piano). Later works written for the same numerical forces are distinguished by superscript indicators (e.g., *Two²* [1989] for two pianos; *Two³* [1991] for shō and conch shells). In their notational layout, the number pieces follow the trend established by *Thirty Pieces for Five Orchestras* in exclusively employing (mostly flexible) time brackets; however, as Pritchett has pointed out, what is new in the number pieces is the almost invariable sparseness of the time brackets' contents.[98] This is clearly evident from a comparison between the opening violin 1 time brackets of *Thirty Pieces for String Quartet* (1983) and *Four* (1989): the former contains, during a maximum duration of one minute, fifteen seconds, thirty separate pitches, notated rhythmically, and punctuated by rests; the latter, in a maximum duration of 37 ½", contains only two (slurred) whole notes.

It would be easy to assume from these introductory comments that the number pieces lack individual identity; nothing could be further from the truth. First, there is the matter of timbre: the resources used in the number pieces range from solo melody instruments (*One⁶* [1990] for violin; *One⁸* [1991] for cello) through duets, trios, quartets, and chamber ensembles (*Three* [1989] for three recorders; *Seven* [1988] for flute, clarinet, violin, viola, cello, percussion, and piano) to large orchestra (*101* [1988]; *108* [1991]). Additionally, some of the instruments chosen—such as the rainsticks of *Four³* (1991), the Japanese shō of *One⁹* (1991), *Two³* (1991), and *Two⁴* (1991), or the conch shells of *Two³*—are timbrally unfamiliar. Second, the timbral *density* of each work is directly related to the number of its performers: in solo pieces, the aural results are often spare, with isolated sounds, or collections of sounds, being framed by silence. But the more instruments Cage employs, the greater the likelihood of overlap between sounds. Third, in a number of works Cage experimented with such features as limited gamuts of pitches, repetition, and (in a manner reminiscent of earlier experiments by Henry Cowell and Lou Harrison) flexible form. Turning again to the example of *Four*, the range of pitches is—in a manner analogous to that of the *String Quartet in Four Parts* (1949–50)—severely restricted, specifically in this case to the two-octave range shared by the four instruments of the string quartet. The tripartite form of the piece can be presented in three ways (B, A+C, A+B+C, these variants lasting respectively ten minutes, twenty minutes, and thirty minutes); and each of the three sections includes a varied repeat in which the "original" instrumental parts are subsequently reiterated, but on another of the instruments (e.g., at the midpoint of B, violin 1 might swap parts with the viola, and violin 2 with the cello). This leads to the same music being played twice but with timbral changes and differing vertical alignments (due to the flexible time brackets) in the "repeat."

Fourth—and most importantly—in every one of the number pieces (as had been the case for all of the post-1950 works) Cage always had a clear and precise idea of the particular aural world he wished to create. Pritchett cites two such examples of composerly choice: in *Twenty-Three* (1988) for string orchestra, "[E]ach part has some of its brackets deleted, so that the size and composition of the ensemble changes from moment to moment." In *Fourteen* (1990) for piano and chamber ensemble, "[T]he piano plays throughout, but the other instruments enter and exit . . . making it a kind of concerto."[99] A particularly noteworthy example is *101* (1988) for orchestra: Cage divides his forces into three basic timbral groups, each of which has a specific function. The largest group—comprising strings, piano, harp, flutes, and clarinets—plays quietly throughout. The almost Ivesian backcloth so created is sporadically punctuated by the second group, the percussion, whose notes are scattered seemingly arbitrarily onto the texture. The remaining winds, together with the brass, appear only twice: once at the beginning of the piece, and once near its end. On each occasion, their music is ragged, in the highest register, and extremely loud; but on their second appearance, the effect is of falling apart rather than coming together. Thus, in the number pieces, computer automation of the compositional process might lead to multiple—and supposedly similar—products. But in reality each work is distinguished by Cage's choices at the precompositional stage.

The one area of Cage's late work left effectively untouched by the computer was his visual art. During his Indian Summer, he continued to make annual visits to Crown Point Press, though in two years (1988 and 1990) these were supplanted by residencies at the Mountain Lake Workshop in Virginia. As Andrew Culver has suggested, Cage's artwork activities were related—albeit obliquely—to the automation of his writings and compositions. Taking the example of his writings, "In the years before Cage had a computer and the operators to work it, he was making large mesostics. . . . Making these was terribly laborious and demanded an incredible discipline. [After automation] the program does all the searching automatically, so the devotional aspect of composing a mesostic is usurped by the machine."[100] Cage therefore sought a channel for the "devotional" side of his work: "His need to undertake difficult tasks was addressed by his making drawings. . . . In place of making mesostics, John had a new outlet for his desire to have a laborious task at hand."[101]

The results of Cage's excursions to California and Virginia were the series titled *HV* (1983), *Ryoku* (1985), *Fire* (1985), *Eninka* (1986), *Déka* (1987), *New River Watercolors* (1988), *Stones* (1989), *River Rocks and Smoke* (1990), *Smoke Weather Stone Weather* (1991), and *HV2* (1992). One feature that links these otherwise disparate series is their common tendency toward experimenting with different materials: alongside the familiar stones and drypoint tools, we now find watercolor, brushes, smoke, fire, and water. The results of these experiments often delighted Cage: for instance, when making the *Eninka* series, he was initially dejected by the "mess" obtained through subjecting thin Japanese paper to fire. His chief printer, Marcia Bartholme, suggested tossing the "crumpled and burned papers into a bath of water." What emerged led Cage to exclaim, "'Oh, it's beautiful! Don't you think it's beautiful? I can't believe it.'"[102] It is therefore entirely appropriate that almost the last series Cage worked on at Crown Point before his death was titled *Without Horizon* (1992; see below). Although Cage could not have known that his life's work was to be completed only eight months later, on August 12, 1992, everything he did was characterized by beauty, optimism, and a unique ability to imagine a future without horizon.

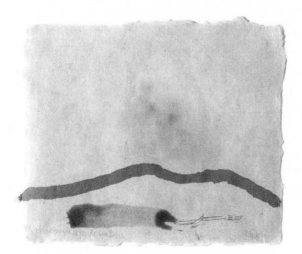

John Cage, Without Horizon 33 *(1992). One in a series of fifty-seven unique aquatints with etching and drypoint on smoked paper printed by Pamela Paulson at Crown Point Press. 7 1/2" x 8 1/2". Used by permission of Crown Point Press.*

POSTLUDE

MORE THAN A DECADE after Cage's death, it is still too early to take full stock of his influence and artistic legacy. Nor can we yet decide whether the opinion voiced by the British music critic Paul Driver—"I doubt if we will go on listening to more than a handful of Cage's hundreds of works"—has any validity (though the number of CDs of Cage's music currently available suggests otherwise).[1] However, some preliminary thoughts on these matters are appropriate in a book such as this.

The work of Arnold Schoenberg has been perpetuated, directly and indirectly, by his pupils, followers, and advocates for almost a century now. Initially through Alban Berg, Anton Webern, and other first-generation Schoenberg students, and latterly through the proponents of serial and post-serial techniques (such as Pierre Boulez and Milton Babbitt) and influential commentators such as Theodor W. Adorno, Schoenberg has had an enormous influence over the music of the last hundred years. Similarly influential, though via slightly different routes, has been the work of Schoenberg's close contemporary, Igor Stravinsky; as Cage himself recognized early on, for the majority of composers working in the twentieth century, the choice—a stark one—was solely between the two S's.

In this traditional, canonic sense of artistic influence, Cage's impact was inevitably limited: he had virtually no direct students or followers, and his aesthetic outlook was too unconventional to be taken seriously by the hardcore musical establishment. As Feldman suggested in 1989, though, when he wrote of "'[t]he rip-off of Cage [being], to some degree, disguised,'"[2] Cage's more general influence has been subtle, at times almost subcutaneous, and often unacknowledged, despite its breadth and depth. On the one hand, many of his innovations were blatantly appropriated by the European avant-garde. On the other hand, his friends and colleagues—including Earle Brown, Morton Feldman, Lou Harrison, and Christian Wolff—as well as numerous later figures from the American

Fluxus movement, the ongoing English and American experimental traditions, and the increasingly ubiquitous tribe of minimalists and postminimalists, have brought Cagean ideas and ideals to public attention. Furthermore, from the 1950s onwards Cage's aesthetic became directly influential through the publication of his writings and the performances of his music. Perhaps even more importantly, he never adopted the self-conscious pomposity and pretentiousness characteristic of all too many contemporary composers: through his approachability, openness, and honesty, Cage made many friends and showed that complex and challenging ideas do not necessarily have to be associated with supposed superiority or artistic aloofness—what one might characterize as "maestro syndrome."

Cage's appeal has always transcended generic boundaries. In the period through the 1960s, artists and dancers often appreciated his work more than did musicians; and since the 1960s, his increasing influence among musicians has not been limited to those working at the radical end of the spectrum. Unlike Stockhausen, Cage was not among the lonely hearts immortalized on the front cover of *Sgt. Pepper;* but Paul McCartney and John Lennon knew of Cage and his work, and in the 1970s—through Yoko Ono—Lennon became a friend and sometime neighbor.

Two recent events give some indication of the degree to which Cage's work has become accepted as a crucial component in contemporary culture. In January 2004, a weekend series of concerts, talks, and films was given by the BBC in London's Barbican Centre. *John Cage Uncaged* played to packed houses, regardless of whether the fare on offer was from the "classic" percussion and prepared-piano period of the 1930s and 1940s or the decidedly more challenging years from 1952 onwards. Indeed, Loré Lixenberg's entirely authentic (though highly amusing) rendition of *Aria* (1958) received a standing ovation. A month or so later, an article by Mark Edwards in the Pop section of the *Sunday Times'* culture supplement opened (*pace* Paul Driver) by stating, "Not only is Cage's music not being forgotten, its influence is clearly spreading." Edwards proceeded to discuss the importance of Cage's work to contemporary popular music, concluding that "[t]he most obvious connection the leaders of the 20th-century classical avant-garde have with those currently at the leading edge of electronica is that their music depends on the arrival of new technologies that allow sounds to be created in new ways or—more importantly—new sounds to be created. Perhaps this is true of all musical development, but Cage and Aphex Twin take this further, adapting existing technologies in an attempt to make the hardware keep up with their ideas. Cage's prepared pianos have an echo in the Twin's self-modified synths."[3]

Cage's ultimate legacy is, to my mind, likely to be twofold: first, he produced a huge and vibrant body of work that—in the words of his London *Times* obituary—challenges "every assumption about the roles of musicians, composers, listeners, even the instruments themselves."[4] Second, and perhaps even more importantly, Cage let sounds be themselves. Thus, to paraphrase something he wrote in 1958 about Satie, in the end it comes down to this: "It's not a question of Cage's relevance. He's indispensable."[5]

NOTES

CHAPTER 1: *The West Coast, 1912–42*

1. Richard Kostelanetz, *Conversing with Cage*, 2d ed. (New York: Routledge, 2003), 1; Cage Family Web Site: www.blakstone.com/Genealogy/WC_TOC.HTM.

2. David Revill, *The Roaring Silence: John Cage, a Life* (London: Bloomsbury, 1992), 17–19.

3. Kostelanetz, *Conversing with Cage*, 1.

4. Ibid.

5. John Cage, *John Cage: Writer*, ed. and intro. Richard Kostelanetz (New York: Cooper Square Press, 2000), 237.

6. Joan Peyser, *Boulez: Composer, Conductor, Enigma* (London: Cassell, 1977), 55.

7. Revill, *Roaring Silence*, 22.

8. John Cage, *Silence* (Middletown, Conn.: Wesleyan University Press, 1961), 6.

9. Revill, *Roaring Silence*, 22.

10. John Cage, *A Year from Monday* (Middletown, Conn.: Wesleyan University Press, 1967), 20.

11. Kostelanetz, *Conversing with Cage*, 2.

12. Calvin Tomkins, *The Bride and the Bachelors* (London: Penguin Books, 1976), 76–77.

13. Thomas S. Hines, "'Then Not Yet "Cage"': The Los Angeles Years, 1912–1938," in *John Cage: Composed in America*, ed. Marjorie Perloff and Charles Junkerman (Chicago: University of Chicago Press, 1994), 74.

14. "Other People Think" is reproduced in Richard Kostelanetz, *John Cage* (London: Allen Lane, 1971), 45–49.

15. Revill, *Roaring Silence*, 32.

16. Ibid., 34.

17. Tomkins, *Bride and the Bachelors*, 78.

18. Hines, "'Then Not Yet "Cage,"'" 79.

19. Tomkins, *Bride and the Bachelors*, 78.

20. Revill, *Roaring Silence*, 36.

21. Mark Katz, *Capturing Sound: How Technology Has Changed Music* (Berkeley: University of California Press, 2004), 113.

22. Kostelanetz, *Conversing with Cage*, 61.

23. Hines, "'Then Not Yet "Cage,"'" 81; Revill, *Roaring Silence*, 33.

24. Christopher Shultis, "Cage and Europe," in *The Cambridge Companion to John Cage*, ed. David Nicholls (Cambridge: Cambridge University Press, 2002), 22–23.

25. Hines, "'Then Not Yet "Cage,"'" 81, 84.

26. Tomkins, *Bride and the Bachelors*, 82.

27. David Nicholls, "Cage and America," in *The Cambridge Companion to John Cage*, ed. David Nicholls (Cambridge: Cambridge University Press, 2002), 12–13.

28. Revill, *Roaring Silence*, 39.

29. Ibid., 40.

30. Cage, *Silence*, 273.

31. Revill, *Roaring Silence*, 40–41.

32. Tomkins, *Bride and the Bachelors*, 81.

33. Cage, *Silence*, 71.

34. Tomkins, *Bride and the Bachelors*, 83.

35. Quoted in Kostelanetz, *John Cage*, 94–95 (this information has never been confirmed by Cage or in any other source).

36. David W. Bernstein, "Music I: To the Late 1940s," in *The Cambridge Companion to John Cage*, ed. David Nicholls (Cambridge: Cambridge University Press, 2002), 63–64.

37. Ibid., 64–66.

38. David Nicholls, *American Experimental Music, 1890–1940* (Cambridge: Cambridge University Press, 1990), 89–133, 134–54, 175–82.

39. Kostelanetz, *Conversing with Cage*, 7.

40. Revill, *Roaring Silence*, 41–44.

41. Kostelanetz, *Conversing with Cage*, 8.

42. Revill, *Roaring Silence*, 41.

43. Michael Hicks, "John Cage's Studies with Schoenberg," *American Music* 8.2 (Summer 1990): 126.

44. Kostelanetz, *Conversing with Cage*, 107.

45. Leta E. Miller, "Henry Cowell and John Cage: Intersections and Influences, 1933–1941," *Journal of the American Musicological Society* 59.1 (Spring 2006): 52–54.

46. Cage, *Silence*, 67–75.

47. Carol J. Oja, *Making Music Modern: New York in the 1920s* (New York: Oxford University Press, 2000), 6.

48. Hicks, "John Cage's Studies with Schoenberg," 127.

49. Arnold Schoenberg, *Style and Idea: Selected Writings of Arnold Schoenberg*, ed. Leonard Stein, trans. Leo Black (London: Faber and Faber, 1975), 388.

50. Quoted in Hicks, "John Cage's Studies with Schoenberg," 129–30.

51. Kostelanetz, *Conversing with Cage*, 5.

52. Cage, *John Cage*, 238.

53. Cage, *Silence*, 33, 85, 93, 261, 265–66, 270–71; John Cage, in conversation with Daniel Charles, *For the Birds* (London: Marion Boyars, 1981), 15, 35–36, 45, 69–73.

54. Kostelanetz, *Conversing with Cage*, 5.

55. Cage, *Silence*, 261.

56. Ibid., 71.

57. Bernstein, "Music I," 66.

58. Kostelanetz, *John Cage*, 81.

59. Kostelanetz, *Conversing with Cage*, 8.

60. Cage, *For the Birds*, 73–74.

61. Kostelanetz, *Conversing with Cage*, 8; Revill, *Roaring Silence*, 51.

62. Cage, *John Cage*, 31, 239.

63. Revill, *Roaring Silence*, 52.

64. Ibid., 55.

65. Ibid., 24.

66. Cage, *Silence*, 264.

67. Leta E. Miller, "Cultural Intersections: John Cage in Seattle (1938–1940)," in *John Cage: Music, Philosophy, and Intention, 1933–1950*, ed. David W. Patterson (New York: Routledge, 2002), 48–50.

68. Ibid., 54–56.

69. The citation of specific lines refers to the layout of the text in Cage, *Silence*, 3–6.

70. Miller, "Henry Cowell and John Cage," 47–48, 91–97.

71. Miller, "Cultural Intersections," 54–56, 59; Nicholls, *American Experimental Music*, 189–91.

72. Cage, *John Cage*, 35.

73. Katz, *Capturing Sound*, 113.

74. Ibid., 100–104, 113.

75. Cage, *John Cage*, 35–37.

76. Revill, *Roaring Silence*, 55.

77. Miller, "Cultural Intersections," 65.

78. John Cage, *Empty Words: Writings '73–'78* (London: Marion Boyars, [1980]), 7–8. See also Stephen Montague, "John Cage at Seventy: An Interview," *American Music* 3.2 (Summer 1985): 209–10.

79. Revill, *Roaring Silence*, 69.

80. Ibid., 70.

81. Miller, "Cultural Intersections," 68.

82. Kostelanetz, *Conversing with Cage*, 9; Revill, *Roaring Silence*, 72–73.

83. Revill, *Roaring Silence*, 78.

CHAPTER 2: *New York #1, 1942–54*

1. David Nicholls, "Cage and America," in *The Cambridge Companion to John Cage*, ed. David Nicholls (Cambridge: Cambridge University Press, 2002), 16–19.

2. Howard Gardner, *Creating Minds* (New York: Basic Books, 1993), 361.

3. John Cage, *Silence* (Middletown, Conn.: Wesleyan University Press, 1961), 12 (this story is also told in several secondary sources); Richard Kostelanetz, *Conversing with Cage*, 2d ed. (New York: Routledge, 2003), 11; David Revill, *The Roaring Silence: John Cage, a Life* (London: Bloomsbury, 1992), 79.

4. Kostelanetz, *Conversing with Cage*, 12; Revill, *Roaring Silence*, 31.

5. Calvin Tomkins, *The Bride and the Bachelors* (London: Penguin Books, 1976), 96.

6. William Brooks, "Music and Society," in *The Cambridge Companion to John Cage*, ed. David Nicholls (Cambridge: Cambridge University Press, 2002), 215.

7. John Cage, *John Cage: Writer*, ed. and intro. Richard Kostelanetz (New York: Cooper Square Press, 2000), 39.

8. Cage, *John Cage*, 40.

9. Thomas S. Hines, "'Then Not Yet "Cage"': The Los Angeles Years, 1912–1938," in *John Cage: Composed in America*, ed. Marjorie Perloff and Charles Junkerman (Chicago: University of Chicago Press, 1994), 99 n.60.

10. Cage, *John Cage*, 40.

11. Revill, *Roaring Silence*, 85.

12. Cage, *John Cage*, 2.

13. Ibid., 5–13.

14. Ibid., 41.

15. David W. Bernstein, "Music I: To the late 1940s," in *The Cambridge Companion to John Cage*, ed. David Nicholls (Cambridge: Cambridge University Press, 2002), 83–84.

16. Leta E. Miller and Fredric Lieberman, *Lou Harrison: Composing a World* (New York: Oxford University Press, 1998), 206–20.

17. Cage, *John Cage*, 8–11.

18. Bernstein, "Music I," 80.

19. Richard Kostelanetz, *John Cage* (London: Allen Lane, 1971), 84–85.

20. Tomkins, *Bride and the Bachelors*, 97.

21. Ibid.

22. Cage, *John Cage*, 239.

23. Kostelanetz, *Conversing with Cage*, 13; Revill, *Roaring Silence*, 87.

24. Cage, *Silence*, 127.

25. Cage, *John Cage*, 41.

26. Ibid.

27. Miller and Lieberman, *Lou Harrison*, 49–50; Kostelanetz, *Conversing with Cage*, 13; David W. Patterson, "Cage and Asia: History and Sources," in *The Cambridge Companion to John Cage*, ed. David Nicholls (Cambridge: Cambridge University Press, 2002), 43.

28. "The East in the West" is reprinted in Cage, *John Cage*, 21–25.

29. Patterson, "Cage and Asia," 44–48.

30. Cage, *John Cage*, 239.

31. Quoted in Patterson, "Cage and Asia," 48.

32. Cage, *John Cage*, 41.

33. Ibid., 13–14.

34. Patterson, "Cage and Asia," 49.

35. Miller and Lieberman, *Lou Harrison*, 37–46.

36. Cage, *John Cage*, 41.

37. Ibid., 41–42.

38. David W. Bernstein, "Cage and High Modernism," in *The Cambridge Companion to John Cage*, ed. David Nicholls (Cambridge: Cambridge University Press, 2002), 187–89; James Pritchett, *The Music of John Cage* (Cambridge: Cambridge University Press, 1993), 44–45.

39. Cage, *John Cage*, 44.

40. Revill, *Roaring Silence*, 92.

41. Cage, *John Cage*, 11.

42. Revill, *Roaring Silence*, 92.

43. Bernstein, "Music I," 83–84.

44. Quoted in Tomkins, *Bride and the Bachelors*, 102–3.

45. Quoted in Pritchett, *Music of John Cage*, 35.

46. Merce Cunningham, "A Collaborative Process between Music and Dance," in *A John Cage Reader*, ed. Peter Gena, Jonathan Brent, and Don Gillespie (New York: C. F. Peters Corporation, 1982), 107–8.

47. On Black Mountain College, see Miller and Lieberman, *Lou Harrison*, 46.

48. Kostelanetz, *John Cage*, 77–84.

49. Revill, *Roaring Silence*, 96.

50. Ibid., 95.

51. Kostelanetz, *Conversing with Cage*, 42.

52. Tomkins, *Bride and the Bachelors*, 103.

53. John Cage, in conversation with Daniel Charles, *For the Birds* (London: Marion Boyars, 1981), 85.

54. Cage, *Silence*, 62–66, 109–26.

55. Ibid., 109.

56. Ibid., 121.

57. Pritchett, *Music of John Cage*, 55.

58. Ibid., 59.

59. Cage, *Silence*, 114.

60. Ibid., 117.

61. Ibid., 109.

62. Pritchett, *Music of John Cage*, 56.

63. Patterson, "Cage and Asia," 53.

64. Ibid., 54.

65. Richard Fleming and William Duckworth, eds., *John Cage at Seventy-Five* (London: Associated University Presses, 1989), 27.

66. Michael Hicks, "John Cage's Studies with Schoenberg," *American Music* 8.2 (Summer 1990): 133–35.

67. Bernstein, "Cage and High Modernism," 189.

68. Cage, *John Cage*, 51.

69. John Cage and Pierre Boulez, *The Boulez-Cage Correspondence*, ed. Jean-Jacques Nattiez, trans. and ed. Robert Samuels (Cambridge: Cambridge University Press, 1993), 49, 55.

70. Ibid., 50.

71. Carolyn A. Jones quoted in David Nicholls, "Getting Rid of the Glue: The Music of the New York School" in *The New York Schools of Music and Visual Arts*, ed. Steven Johnson (New York: Routledge, 2002), 18.

72. Feldman quoted in ibid., 20.

73. Quoted in Tomkins, *Bride and the Bachelors*, 108.

74. Quoted in Nicholls, "Getting Rid of the Glue," 25.

75. Tomkins, *Bride and the Bachelors*, 108.

76. Quoted in Cage, *Silence*, 71.

77. Revill, *Roaring Silence*, 103.

78. Cage and Boulez, *Correspondence*, 48.

79. Bernstein, "Cage and High Modernism," 193.

80. Cage and Boulez, *Correspondence*, 78.

81. Ibid.

82. Ibid.

83. Bernstein, "Cage and High Modernism," 199.

84. Cage and Boulez, *Correspondence*, 94; Bernstein, "Cage and High Modernism," 199–201.

85. Kostelanetz, *Conversing with Cage*, 68.

86. Bernstein, "Cage and High Modernism," 202.

87. Pritchett, *Music of John Cage*, 74.

88. Ibid., 74–75.

89. Bernstein, "Cage and High Modernism," 203–8; Pritchett, *Music of John Cage*, 78–88.

90. Quoted in Tomkins, *Bride and the Bachelors*, 112.

91. Cage and Boulez, *Correspondence*, 97.

92. Ibid., 112.

93. Kostelanetz, *Conversing with Cage*, 8.

94. Cage and Boulez, *Correspondence*, 118.

95. Quoted in Joan Peyser, *Boulez: Composer, Conductor, Enigma* (London: Cassell, 1977), 97.

96. Quoted in ibid., 84.

97. Quoted in ibid., 107.

98. Quoted in Tomkins, *Bride and the Bachelors*, 109.

99. Quoted in ibid., 108.

100. Pritchett, *Music of John Cage*, 69.

101. Cage, *Silence*, 129–30.

102. Quoted in Tomkins, *Bride and the Bachelors*, 114.

103. Tomkins, *Bride and the Bachelors*, 114; Cage, *For the Birds*, 85–86.

104. Cage and Boulez, *Correspondence*, 131.

105. See Nicholls, "Getting Rid of the Glue."

106. Pritchett, *Music of John Cage*, 92.

107. Cage, *Silence*, 60–61.

108. Tomkins, *Bride and the Bachelors*, 107.

109. Leta E. Miller, "Cage's Collaborations," in *The Cambridge Companion to John Cage*, ed. David Nicholls (Cambridge: Cambridge University Press, 2002), 151.

110. Ibid.

111. Cage, *John Cage*, 43.

112. Kostelanetz, *Conversing with Cage*, 71.

113. Cage, *Silence*, 98.

114. Cage, *For the Birds*, 115.

115. John Cage, *A Year from Monday* (Middletown, Conn.: Wesleyan University Press, 1967), 98.

116. Cage, *Silence*, 8.

117. Kostelanetz, *Conversing with Cage*, 69, 70.

118. Ibid., 70.

119. Ibid.

120. Gardner, *Creating Minds*, 361.

CHAPTER 3: *Stony Point, 1954–70*

1. Richard Kostelanetz, *Conversing with Cage*, 2d ed. (New York: Routledge, 2003), 15.

2. Ibid.

3. David Revill, *The Roaring Silence: John Cage, A Life* (London: Bloomsbury, 1992), 148.

4. See William Duckworth, *Talking Music* (New York: Schirmer Books, 1995), 16–17.

5. Kostelanetz, *Conversing with Cage*, 15.

6. Ibid., 16–17.

7. Ibid., 17.

8. Ibid., 16.

9. Arthur Waley, *Translations from the Chinese* (New York: Alfred A. Knopf, 1941), 79.

10. See David Nicholls, "Towards Infinity: Cage in the 1950s and 1960s," in *The Cambridge Companion to John Cage*, ed. David Nicholls (Cambridge: Cambridge University Press, 2002), 100–108.

11. Quoted in Richard Kostelanetz, *John Cage* (London: Allen Lane, 1971), 153.

12. John Cage, *Silence* (Middletown, Conn.: Wesleyan University Press, 1961), 276.

13. John Cage and Pierre Boulez, *The Boulez-Cage Correspondence*, ed. Jean-Jacques Nattiez, trans. and ed. Robert Samuels (Cambridge: Cambridge University Press, 1993), 143.

14. James Pritchett, *The Music of John Cage* (Cambridge: Cambridge University Press, 1993), 95–104.

15. See Amy C. Beal, "The Army, the Airwaves, and the Avant-Garde: American Classical Music in Postwar West Germany," *American Music* 21.4 (Winter 2003): 487–501.

16. Joan Peyser, *Boulez: Composer, Conductor, Enigma* (London: Cassell, 1977), 107.

17. Calvin Tomkins, *The Bride and the Bachelors* (London: Penguin Books, 1976), 125.

18. Pritchett, *Music of John Cage*, 55.

19. Cage, *Silence*, 146–92; for the two passages in the "Juilliard Lecture," see 103, 100–101.

20. Ibid., 148.

21. John Cage, *John Cage: Writer*, ed. and intro. Richard Kostelanetz (New York: Cooper Square Press, 2000), 55–56.

22. Ibid., 56.

23. Kostelanetz, *Conversing with Cage*, 167.

24. Revill, *Roaring Silence*, 190.

25. Tomkins, *Bride and the Bachelors*, 127.

26. Pritchett, *Music of John Cage*, 112–23.

27. Ibid., 110.

28. John Holzaepfel, "Cage and Tudor," in *The Cambridge Companion to John Cage*, ed. David Nicholls (Cambridge: Cambridge University Press, 2002), 176–85.

29. Quoted in Tomkins, *Bride and the Bachelors*, 128.

30. Christopher Shultis, "Cage and Europe," in *The Cambridge Companion to John Cage*, ed. David Nicholls (Cambridge: Cambridge University Press, 2002), 33.

31. For "Composition as Process," see Cage, *Silence*, 18–56.

32. Shultis, "Cage and Europe," 35.

33. Cage, *Silence*, 18.

34. Shultis, "Cage and Europe," 36–38.

35. Cage, *Silence*, 67–75.

36. Shultis, "Cage and Europe," 39.

37. Cage, *Silence*, 69.

38. Ibid., 68–69, 71.

39. Ibid., 74–75.

40. Ibid., 73.

41. Ibid., 75.

42. Quoted in David Nicholls, "Getting Rid of the Glue: The Music of the New York School," in *The New York Schools of Music and Visual Arts*, ed. Steven Johnson (New York: Routledge, 2002), 49.

43. Ibid., 47–50.

44. Cage, *Silence*, 261–73; John Cage, *A Year from Monday* (Middletown, Conn.: Wesleyan University Press, 1967), 133–40.

45. Cage, *Silence*, 260.

46. Tomkins, *Bride and the Bachelors*, 130.

47. Cage, *Silence*, 273.

48. Pritchett, *Music of John Cage*, 128–29.

49. Ibid., 126–37.

50. Cage, *John Cage*, 60.

51. Cage, *Silence*, 195–259.

52. Tomkins, *Bride and the Bachelors*, 130–33; Revill, *Roaring Silence*, 194–96.

53. Kostelanetz, *Conversing with Cage*, 21–22.

54. Cage, *Silence*, xi.

55. Cage, *Year from Monday*, 112–19, 120–32.

56. Leta E. Miller, "Cage, Cunningham, and Collaborators: The Odyssey of *Variations V*," *Musical Quarterly* 85.3 (Fall 2001): 550.

57. Kostelanetz, *Conversing with Cage*, 126.

58. Cage, *Silence*, xi.

59. David W. Patterson, "Words and Writings," in *The Cambridge Companion to John Cage*, ed. David Nicholls (Cambridge: Cambridge University Press, 2002), 85–87.

60. Cage, *Silence*, 260–73.

61. Pritchett, *Music of John Cage*, 143.

62. Ibid.

63. Ibid., 144.

64. Ibid.

65. Cage, *Year from Monday*, ix.

66. Ibid., 3–20, 52–69, 145–62; John Cage, *M: Writings '67–'72* (London: Calder and Boyars, 1973), 3–25, 57–84, 96–116, 193–217 (the last two segments are from 1970–71 and 1971–72).

67. Pritchett, *Music of John Cage*, 55.

68. Cage, *Year from Monday*, 3.

69. Ibid., 4–5.

70. Tomkins, *Bride and the Bachelors*, 267.

71. Leta E. Miller, "Cage's Collaborations," in *The Cambridge Companion to John Cage*, ed. David Nicholls (Cambridge: Cambridge University Press, 2002), 160.

72. Miller, "Cage, Cunningham, and Collaborators," 557–59.

73. Miller, "Cage's Collaborations," 163.

74. Cage quoted in Stephen Husarik, "John Cage and Lejaren Hiller: HPSCHD, 1969," in *American Music* 1.2 (Summer 1983): 11.

75. Ibid., 9–10.

76. Ibid., 11.

77. Quoted in ibid., 14.

78. Ibid.

79. Quoted in ibid., 2. See also Miller, "Cage's Collaborations"; and Miller, "Cage, Cunningham, and Collaborators."

80. Cage, *Silence*, 14–15.

81. Kathan Brown, "Visual Art," in *The Cambridge Companion to John Cage*, ed. David Nicholls (Cambridge: Cambridge University Press, 2002), 112–13.

82. Pritchett, *Music of John Cage*, 138.

83. Salzman quoted in Kostelanetz, *John Cage*, 150–51.

84. Brown quoted in Nicholls, "Towards Infinity," 108.

CHAPTER 4: *New York #2, 1970–92*

1. John Cage, *Year from Monday* (Middletown, Conn.: Wesleyan University Press, 1967), ix–x.

2. John Cage, in conversation with Daniel Charles, *For the Birds* (London: Marion Boyars, 1981), 62 n.2.

3. Ibid., 187.

4. David Revill, *The Roaring Silence: John Cage, A Life* (London: Bloomsbury, 1992), 233, 263.

5. Quoted in ibid., 179.

6. Quoted in Cage, *Year from Monday*, 145.

7. Stephen Montague, "John Cage at Seventy: An Interview," *American Music* 3.2 (Summer 1985): 207.

8. Quoted in David Nicholls, "Avant-Garde and Experimental Music," in *The Cam-*

bridge History of American Music, ed. David Nicholls (Cambridge: Cambridge University Press, 1998), 532.

9. James Pritchett, *The Music of John Cage* (Cambridge: Cambridge University Press, 1993), 162.

10. John Cage, *John Cage: Writer,* ed. and intro. Richard Kostelanetz (New York: Cooper Square Press, 2000), 93.

11. Ibid., 95.

12. Cage, *For the Birds,* 183–84 n.1.

13. Revill, *Roaring Silence,* 207–8.

14. John Cage, *M: Writings '67–'72* (London: Calder and Boyars, 1973), [ix].

15. On Cage and Thoreau, see Christopher Shultis, *Silencing the Sounded Self: John Cage and the American Experimental Tradition* (Boston: Northeastern University Press, 1998), esp. 29–58.

16. Revill, *Roaring Silence,* 220.

17. Cage, *M,* 70.

18. Cage, *For the Birds,* 59.

19. William Brooks, "Music II: From the Late 1960s," in *The Cambridge Companion to John Cage,* ed. David Nicholls (Cambridge: Cambridge University Press, 2002), 132; Pritchett, *Music of John Cage,* 183–84.

20. Cage, *John Cage,* 102.

21. Ibid., 104.

22. Pritchett, *Music of John Cage,* 189.

23. Richard Kostelanetz, *Conversing with Cage,* 2d ed. (New York: Routledge, 2003), 89.

24. Ibid., 90.

25. Ibid., 87.

26. John Cage, *Empty Words: Writings '73–'78* (London: Marion Boyars, [1980]), 3–5 (quote on 5).

27. Ibid., 3.

28. Ibid.

29. Kostelanetz, *Conversing with Cage,* 105.

30. Brooks, "Music II," 134.

31. Kostelanetz, *Conversing with Cage,* 245.

32. Cage, *John Cage,* 99.

33. Pritchett, *Music of John Cage,* 199.

34. Cage, *John Cage,* 107.

35. Revill, *Roaring Silence,* 256.

36. Quoted in ibid.

37. Kostelanetz, *Conversing with Cage,* 30.

38. Cage, *M,* 35–56 (quote on [ix]).

39. Ibid., [ix].

40. Ibid.

41. Ibid., [x].

42. Cage, *Empty Words*, 11–77.

43. Kostelanetz, *Conversing with Cage*, 146.

44. Revill, *Roaring Silence*, 249.

45. Kostelanetz, *Conversing with Cage*, 147.

46. Ibid., 149.

47. Cage, *Empty Words*, 12, 76.

48. Kostelanetz, *Conversing with Cage*, 146.

49. Cage, *John Cage*, 98.

50. Kostelanetz, *Conversing with Cage*, 147.

51. *Concise Oxford Dictionary*, 5th ed., 601.

52. For "Song," see Cage, *M*, 86–91; for "Another Song," see John Cage, *X: Writings '79–'82* (London: Marion Boyars, 1987), 103–7.

53. Cage, *John Cage*, 196.

54. Cage, *M*, 94 (quote on [ix]).

55. Ibid., 4–211 passim (quote on [x]).

56. Ibid., [ix].

57. Cage, *X*, 1.

58. Pritchett, *Music of John Cage*, 159.

59. Brooks, "Music II," 139. See also Revill, *Roaring Silence*, 275.

60. Kostelanetz, *Conversing with Cage*, 161.

61. Ibid., 153.

62. Cage, *Empty Words*, 135.

63. Ibid., 137–76.

64. Cage, *X*, 1–49, 173–87.

65. Ibid., 173.

66. Cage, *Empty Words*, 136.

67. Revill, *Roaring Silence*, 265.

68. Pritchett, *Music of John Cage*, 179.

69. Revill, *Roaring Silence*, 267.

70. Ibid.

71. Kathan Brown, "Visual Art," in *The Cambridge Companion to John Cage*, ed. David Nicholls (Cambridge: Cambridge University Press, 2002), 109.

72. Ibid. For examples of this work, see Kathan Brown, *John Cage—Visual Art: To Sober and Quiet the Mind* (San Francisco: Crown Point Press, 2000); and *Writings through John Cage's Music, Poetry, and Art*, ed. David W. Bernstein and Christopher Hatch (Chicago: University of Chicago Press, 2001).

73. Brown, *John Cage—Visual Art*, 47.

74. See Pritchett, *Music of John Cage*, 188–89, 191.

75. Revill, *Roaring Silence*, 274.

76. Brown, *John Cage—Visual Art*, 87.

77. Ibid., 92.

78. Ibid., 96.

79. Revill, *Roaring Silence*, 264.

80. Cage, *John Cage*, 165–76, 183–94, 229–35, 251–54.

81. *John Cage at Seventy-Five*, ed. Richard Fleming and William Duckworth (London: Associated University Presses, 1989), 119–208.

82. John Cage, *Composition in Retrospect* (Cambridge, Mass.: Exact Change, 1993), 73–171.

83. John Cage, *MethodStructureIntentionDisciplineNotationIndeterminacyInterpenetration-ImitationDevotionCircumstancesVariableStructureNonunderstandingContingencyInconsistency-Performance (I–VI)* (Cambridge, Mass.: Harvard University Press, 1990).

84. Revill, *Roaring Silence*, 286.

85. Cage, *I–VI*, 9.

86. Bernstein and Hatch, *Writings through John Cage's Music, Poetry, and Art*, 197.

87. The programs are listed in ibid., 194–95.

88. Pritchett, *Music of John Cage*, 186.

89. Revill, *Roaring Silence*, 272.

90. See Pritchett, *Music of John Cage*, 186–89.

91. Cage, *John Cage*, 245.

92. Quoted in Revill, *Roaring Silence*, 283.

93. Bernstein and Hatch, *Writings through John Cage's Music, Poetry, and Art*, 205.

94. Revill, *Roaring Silence*, 283 (partly quoting Cage).

95. Pritchett, *Music of John Cage*, 197.

96. Cage, *John Cage*, 213–18.

97. Revill, *Roaring Silence*, 293.

98. Pritchett, *Music of John Cage*, 200–202.

99. Ibid., 202.

100. Bernstein and Hatch, *Writings through John Cage's Music, Poetry, and Art*, 196.

101. Ibid.

102. Quoted in Brown, *John Cage—Visual Art*, 100, 104.

POSTLUDE

1. Paul Driver, "Artist of the Arbitrary," *Sunday (London) Times*, August 16, 1992, sec. 7, p. 4.

2. Quoted in David Nicholls, "Getting Rid of the Glue: The Music of the New York School," in *The New York Schools of Music and Visual Arts*, ed. Steven Johnson (New York: Routledge, 2002), 49.

3. Mark Edwards, "Changing of the Avant-Garde," *Sunday (London) Times*, February 29, 2004, magazine section, p. 10.

4. "John Cage," (London) *Times*, August 14, 1992, 22.

5. John Cage, *Silence* (Middletown, Conn.: Wesleyan University Press, 1961), 82.

SELECTED WORKS

+ indicates a work written specifically for dance accompaniment
† indicates an unpublished work

Sonata for Clarinet (1933)
Quartet for percussion (1935)
Trio for percussion (1936)
Metamorphosis for piano (1938)
Imaginary Landscape No. 1 for variable-speed turntables, frequency recordings, muted piano, and cymbal (1939)
First Construction (in Metal) for six percussionists (1939)
Second Construction for four percussionists (1940)
Bacchanale for prepared piano (1940) +
Living Room Music for percussion and speech quartet (1940)
Double Music (co-composed with Lou Harrison) for four percussionists (1940)
Third Construction for four percussionists (1941)
Imaginary Landscape No. 2 (March No. 1) for five percussionists (1942)
Imaginary Landscape No. 3 for six percussionists (1942)
The City Wears a Slouch Hat for five percussionists (1942)
Credo in Us for four percussionists (1942) +
The Wonderful Widow of Eighteen Springs for voice and closed piano (1942)
Amores for prepared piano and three percussionists (1943)
Our Spring Will Come for prepared piano (1943) +
She Is Asleep, consisting of *Quartet* for twelve tom-toms, *Duet* for voice and prepared piano, and *A Room* for piano or prepared piano (1943)
The Perilous Night for prepared piano (1944)
A Book of Music for two prepared pianos (1944)
Four Walls for voice and piano (1944) +
Daughters of the Lonesome Isle for prepared piano (1945) +
Mysterious Adventure for prepared piano (1945) +
Three Dances for two prepared pianos (1945)
Two Pieces for piano (1946)
The Seasons for orchestra or piano (1947) +

Sonatas and Interludes for prepared piano (1946–48)

Suite for toy piano or piano (1948) +

String Quartet in Four Parts for string quartet (1949–50)

Sixteen Dances for flute, trumpet, four percussion, violin, cello, and piano (1950–51) +

Concerto for Prepared Piano and Orchestra (1950–51)

Imaginary Landscape No. 4 (March No. 2) for twelve radios (1951)

Music of Changes for piano (1951)

Imaginary Landscape No. 5 for any forty-two recordings (1952) +

Water Music for a pianist (1952)

Black Mountain Piece, multimedia event (1952) †

4' 33" for any instrument(s) (1952)

Williams Mix for one eight-track or four two-track tape recorders (1952)

Music for Piano 4–19 (1953)

34' 46.776" for a pianist (1954)

31' 57.9864" for a pianist (1954)

26' 1.1499" for a string player (1953–55)

Music for Piano 21–36 and *37–52* (1955)

Speech 1955 for five radios and a newsreader (1955)

27' 10.554" for a percussionist (1956)

Music for Piano 53–68 and *69–84* (1956)

Radio Music for one to eight radios (1956)

Winter Music for one to twenty pianos (1957)

Concert for piano and orchestra, including *Solo for Piano* (1957–58)

Variations I for any number of players, any means (1958)

Fontana Mix for tape (1958)

Aria for voice (1958)

Theatre Piece for one to eight performers (1960)

Cartridge Music for amplified sounds (1961)

Variations II for any number of players, any means (1961)

Atlas Eclipticalis for any ensemble drawn from eighty-six instrumentalists (1962)

0' 00" (4' 33" No. 2) for solo performer (1962)

Variations IV for any number of players, any means (1963)

Rozart Mix for tape loops (1965)

Variations V, audiovisual performance (1965)

Musicircus, mixed-media event (1967) †

Reunion for electronics (1967) †

HPSCHD (co-composed with Lejaren Hiller) for one to seven amplified harpsichords, one to fifty-one tapes (1967–69) †

Cheap Imitation for piano (1969) +; for orchestra (1972); for violin (1977)

Song Books (Solos for Voice 3–92) (1970)

Score (40 Drawings by Thoreau) and 23 Parts for any instruments (1974)

Etudes Australes for piano (1974–75)

Child of Tree for a percussionist using amplified plant materials (1975)

Lecture on the Weather for twelve voices and tape (1975)

Renga for seventy-eight voices or instruments (1976)

Apartment House 1776, mixed-media event for any ensemble (1976); excerpts
    arranged for violin and piano (1986)

Etudes Boreales for cello and/or piano (1978)

Some of "The Harmony of Maine" for organist with three to six assistants (1978)

Hymns and Variations for twelve amplified voices (1979)

_____, _____ _____ *circus on* _____ for any ensemble (1979); realized as
    Roaratorio, an Irish Circus on Finnegans Wake for tape (1979)

30 Pieces for 5 Orchestras (1981)

30 Pieces for String Quartet (1983)

Ryoanji for voices, flute, oboe, trombone, double bass, percussion, and
    small orchestra (1983–85)

Essay for tape (1986)

Music for _____ for variable chamber ensemble (1984–87)

Two for flute and piano (1987)

Europeras 1 and 2 for nineteen voices, twenty-one players, and tape (1987)

One for piano (1987)

101 for orchestra (1988)

Seven for flute, clarinet, violin, viola, cello, percussion, and piano (1988)

Twenty-Three for string orchestra (1988)

Four for string quartet (1989)

Three for three recorders (1989)

Fourteen for piano and chamber ensemble (1990)

One^6 for violin (1990)

Europeras 3 and 4 for six voices, two pianos, twelve Victrolas, and tape (1990)

Europera 5 for two voices, Victrola, and tape/TV/radio (1991)

One^8 for cello (1991)

Four^3 for one or two pianos, rainsticks, and violin/oscillator (1991)

One^9 for shō (1991)

Two^3 for shō and conch shells (1991)

Two^4 for violin and piano/shō (1991)

Twenty-Eight for wind ensemble (1991)

Twenty-Six for twenty-six violins (1991)

Twenty-Eight, Twenty-Six, and Twenty-Nine for orchestra (1991)

One^{10} for violin (1992)

Two^6 for violin and piano (1992)

FOR FURTHER READING

This book can serve only as an introduction to Cage's life and work; further reading is therefore essential. The following list does not include all items cited in the text and notes, only those that are particularly recommended. In addition, see Paul van Emmerik's excellent website *A John Cage Compendium*, www.xs4all .nl/~cagecomp/.

Bernstein, David W., and Christopher Hatch, eds. *Writings through John Cage's Music, Poetry, and Art.* Chicago: University of Chicago Press, 2001.

Brown, Kathan. *John Cage—Visual Art: To Sober and Quiet the Mind.* San Francisco: Crown Point Press, 2000.

Cage, John. *John Cage: Writer.* Ed. and intro. Richard Kostelanetz. New York: Cooper Square Press, 2000.

———. *Silence.* Middletown, Conn.: Wesleyan University Press, 1961.

———, in conversation with Daniel Charles. *For the Birds.* London: Marion Boyars, 1981.

Fleming, Richard, and William Duckworth, eds. *John Cage at Seventy-Five.* London: Associated University Presses, 1989.

Kostelanetz, Richard. *Conversing with Cage.* 2d ed. New York: Routledge, 2003.

———. *John Cage.* London: Allen Lane, 1971.

Nicholls, David, ed. *The Cambridge Companion to John Cage.* Cambridge: Cambridge University Press, 2002.

Pritchett, James. *The Music of John Cage.* Cambridge: Cambridge University Press, 1993.

Revill, David. *The Roaring Silence: John Cage, A Life.* London: Bloomsbury, 1992.

Tomkins, Calvin. *The Bride and the Bachelors.* London: Penguin Books, 1976.

SUGGESTED LISTENING

MUCH OF CAGE'S OUTPUT is currently available on CD. The Mode and Wergo labels have released a large number of Cage recordings, including some of historical interest, such as the 1958 *Twenty-Five-Year Retrospective Concert* (WER 6247-2), which reproduces all the accompanying essays and photographs from the original Avakian LP edition, and Cage's performances of his text works, including that accompanying the recording of *Roaratorio*, as well as the complete *Diary: How to Improve the World (You Will Only Make Matters Worse)* (WER 6912-2).

Mdg has issued a multivolume set of Cage's complete keyboard music, performed by Steffen Schleiermacher, while Naxos publishes CDs of his music for prepared piano. Other items of notable interest elsewhere in the catalog include David Tudor's performance of the *Music of Changes* (on Hat Noir HATN133); a live recording of the notorious New York Philharmonic rendition of *Atlas Eclipticalis* with *Winter Music* (on *Bernstein Live:* Special Editions NYP 2012/13, disc 9); the first performance of *Variations IV* (on Legacy; no catalog number); *Roaratorio* (mode 28/29); and *Europera 3* and *Europera 4*, performed by Long Beach Opera (mode 38/39).

Listeners requiring a short aural overview of Cage's music (including two very different performances of the *Concert for Piano and Orchestra*) should try the *Twenty-Five-Year Retrospective Concert* (details above), followed by *The Barton Workshop Plays John Cage* (Etcetera KTC3002). Between them, these two releases include representative selections covering almost the whole of Cage's creative life, from the early *Sonata for Clarinet* right through to the late "number pieces."

INDEX

135

AMERICAN

Composers

Lou Harrison
Leta E. Miller and Fredric Lieberman
John Cage
David Nicholls

DAVID NICHOLLS is a professor of music at the University of Southampton. He is the author of *American Experimental Music, 1890–1940* and editor of *The Cambridge History of American Music* and *The Cambridge Companion to John Cage*.

The University of Illinois Press
is a founding member of the
Association of American University Presses.

Composed in 9.5/13 Janson Text
with Meta and Janson display
by Jim Proefrock
at the University of Illinois Press
Designed by Copenhaver Cumpston
Manufactured by Thomson-Shore, Inc.

UNIVERSITY OF ILLINOIS PRESS
1325 South Oak Street   Champaign, IL 61820-6903
www.press.uillinois.edu

M,